CULTURES
AND
SOCIAL INTELLIGENCE

C. Margaret Hall

Cultures and Social Intelligence *is a guide to discovering the power and complexities of cultures and social influences, as well as the impacts they have on our freedom and opportunities. This book is dedicated to readers who want to better themselves, their accomplishments, and the world we live in.*

Table of Contents

The Power and Complexities of Cultures

Social Intelligence and Cultures

The Power and Complexities of Cultures

I. Cultures as Civilizations

When we consider cultures as civilizations, many basic questions come to mind. For example, how do we define cultures? What do we understand cultures to be? How much do cultures influence our lives? What is the nature of the power and complexities of cultures? Can we avoid or escape from cultural influences? What differences do cultures make in populations? How are cultures related to civilizations and social changes? These are important and compelling existential issues which we need to consider and act upon if we are to live fully.

Cultures and Social Intelligence answers these questions by introducing social intelligence perspectives to deepen our understanding of cultures. For example, we approach our goals by rethinking our ideas about the power and complexities of cultures, and by exploring how social intelligence helps us to see cultures differently. After this, we may choose to make changes where needed, especially in relation to those cultures and cultural bonds that influence us the most.

Even though social intelligence is used more deliberately in the forthcoming **Social Intelligence and Cultures** section of *Cultures and Social Intelligence*, as well as in the **Changing Cultures** section, we start here to develop a sense of what social intelligence is—and the differences that social intelligence makes—by initially viewing cultures from the broad social perspectives used most in social intelligence. For example, our social intelligence derives largely from examining the five major social influences of families, beliefs, social classes, cultures, and societies, which helps us to define cultures, as well as to understand and change cultures.

Cultures are made up of values, ideas, beliefs, ideals, expectations, stereotypes, images, knowledge, religions, sciences, legal systems, meanings, symbols, goals, dreams, and assumptions. This list of different aspects of cultures is not exhaustive, and societies have varied ways to express, understand, and use their cultures. Some cultures are similar to each other, while others are dramatically different. Consequently, there are endless possibilities and varieties of cultures, as well as infinite ways to interpret cultures.

For the purposes of *Cultures and Social Intelligence*, we acknowledge that cultures are social products which we cannot ignore, because they permeate everything we think and do. For example, cultures provide us with meanings which help us to make sense of our everyday lives, and at the same time they are foundations of our civilizations.

When we consider cultures as civilizations, we usually single out some of the dominant values that different societies and contrasting civilizations express. A socially intelligent way to proceed in this difficult task is to examine patterns in the values of families, beliefs, social classes, cultures, and societies—the five major social influences that impact our thoughts and actions the most. Because these five major social influences are interrelated, we understand cultures more fully when we use the four other major social influences to see cultures' power and complexities.

As we start our journeys to understand the deepest impacts of cultures, as well as to play more significant roles in changing our relationships to cultures that dominate our lives, we examine the nature of human nature, and how cultures grow and develop. We familiarize ourselves with the immense diversification of cultures through time and place, for example, by giving special attention to cultures that we may consider to be barbaric or refined. When we examine cultures in different time perspectives, we see both continuities and contrasts in cultures, as well as make more effective decisions about what our new or future cultures could be, especially with regard to their dominant values.

One goal in assessing the power and complexities of cultures is to simplify the power and complexities sufficiently, so that we are not overwhelmed by them in our everyday decision-making and actions. Furthermore, we get a clearer sense of the significance of cultures in our lives, when we realize how cultures affect our ongoing consideration and attention to our social situations.

For example, considering our most basic family needs helps us become more aware of which values are most constructive to pass on to members of our youngest generations, and how we can accomplish these communications most effectively. Societal cultures are sources of our families' cultures and vice versa, so we assess their interrelatedness by finding shared and unshared patterns in both our families' and societies' cultures.

The Nature of Human Nature

Because no one has a definitive answer to the question of what the nature of human nature is, we necessarily make assumptions about human nature based on our limited experiences and incomplete knowledge. For example, we may try to understand others by getting to know ourselves more fully, especially by becoming increasingly aware of how we respond to others as we grow to maturity.

However, it is not socially intelligent to generalize solely from our most deeply lived experiences, especially if we do not practice understanding others from their points of view. For example, only when we are aware of rich varieties of human diversity can we effectively question the assumptions we habitually make about the nature of human nature, thereby deepening our understanding about who we are and what we could be.

Cultures express and reflect the nature of human nature. Cultures are made up of social facts that show us how we honor or dishonor our own families and beliefs, for example, as well as how we often thoughtlessly uphold many injustices related to our social class values. We find that our cultures are rife with contradictions and hypocrisies. However, these anomalies are perhaps more accurately thought of as suggesting broader

3

ranges of possibilities in the nature of human nature than we had previously considered.

Our interests in increasing our social intelligence often start with examining family influences on the qualities of our lives. By identifying facts in patterns of family interactions in individual families and social trends in families, we see that the emotional bonds of families are powerful and complex. For example, our families may influence us to go in particular directions for decades, especially in developing significant cultural interests such as religions or education. In many respects we are who we are not because of our instincts, but because of our beliefs and value choices, which we often acquire through our families.

Due to the fact that patterns of family interactions are relatively easy to observe—especially during crises such as births, marriages, and deaths—we see that our whole beings are sometimes caught up in our families' most emotional issues that pressure us to decide which family cultures to uphold, which family beliefs to use as our own, and which societal values to include in our family cultures. The power and complexities of these social, emotional, and cultural influences, and their effects on our life outcomes, suggest that we are interdependent social beings, and that the reciprocity of these social, emotional, and cultural influences affects everything we do individually and collectively.

Another aspect of the nature of human nature that we need to consider in our quests to understand cultures, is the extent to which we need other people to make progressive changes in our societies. For example, when we share values directly with others, we are more effective in reaching our goals, than if we work in isolation. Furthermore, embracing social diversity in our actions allows us to more easily renew ourselves, as well as strengthen our intentions to increase the common good and social justice. When we value others' contributions, we work together more harmoniously for the benefit of communities as well as ourselves.

I. Cultures as Civilizations

Social intelligence helps us to keep positive and productive aspects of human nature in mind as we go about our daily lives. When we acknowledge and honor our dependencies on others, for example, we are more inclined to take care of our communities or societies, in addition to meeting our own needs. Even though each of us needs to assume some family responsibilities, we should also focus our energies and talents on broad social issues—such as changing our cultures—so that our cultures become constructive rather than destructive social influences.

For example, when we experience others' resistance to our plans for changing cultures, we benefit from reassessing our understanding of human nature. Consequently, we may decide to be more patient with others' resistance, or to persist in chipping away at the many forms of resistance to cultural innovations that we encounter. In any event, we increase our social intelligence when we interact with others, especially when we work toward shared goals like making our cultures more responsive to the real needs people have to live fully, and to contribute to our communities and societies.

The issue of the nature of human nature necessarily remains an open question which we continue to rework, depending on others' experiences and knowledge as well as our own. When we decide to become more socially intelligent, for example, we often meet other goals more effectively, because we continue to address the significant issue of whether we are sufficiently objective in understanding the nature of human nature in our daily exchanges.

Cultures Grow

Cultures grow and develop through reciprocal rituals that maintain our social institutions—families, religions, economies, education, and political systems—and form foundations for our societies. Cultures are crucial complex social realities, because they give us reasons to act together to preserve our societies, and provide justifications as well as motivations for our behavior. Cultures are necessary for our survival because we need cultural symbols to think clearly, as well as to formulate ideas and ideals, especially in deciding which worlds we want to create through our cultures. For example, cultures allow us to make particular value choices in our decision-making and commitments, so that we express our preferred ideas, ideals, and values through our actions.

Our earliest societies developed from families, tribes, and clans, where people frequently shared similar cultural ideas and ideals. For example, traditions and customs established ways to accomplish vital tasks, which were continued from generation to generation. Consequently, family cultures grew bigger, with the result that they gradually became community and national cultures. Thus, these new cultures had more broadly shared values that served the needs of large groups of families, clans, communities, and societies. However, because these early wider cultures were often homogeneous, their populations thought and acted in similar ways—that is, according to their own traditions and customs—over long periods of time.

When more individuals and groups traveled long distances—between societies as well as between communities—they passed on their original cultures to the communities and societies they encountered. Although geographically distant communities and societies resisted changing their values and cultures, more diverse values and ideals were exchanged and absorbed more or less automatically and sometimes peacefully.

Consequently, our cultures gradually became much more complex than they had been, at the same time continuing to have powerful impacts on the qualities of life of their populations. For example, as national populations became larger, cultures were increasingly thought of as foundations of societies, and as ways to hold societies together.

From the broad perspectives of social intelligence—especially from the points of view of families, beliefs, social classes, cultures, and societies—cultures grew larger and become more diverse through time. As this happened, cultures also maintained considerable influences over how necessary tasks are accomplished in societies. For example, cultures are sources of our willingness and motives to perform tasks in societies which hold societies together sufficiently to survive and prosper.

However, the fact that not all societies survive and thrive equally makes us realize that some cultures perform more vital functions than others, or that some cultures nurture more constructive values than others. Social intelligence responds to concerns we have about which values we need to cultivate in our cultures, in order to grow and develop cultures that enhance our possibilities of both surviving and prospering meaningfully through time.

Social intelligence also encourages us to be extremely cautious about the hazards of creating destructive cultures. For example, social intelligence shows us that destructive cultures may ultimately jeopardize the survival of their societies and other societies. However, to the extent that we choose to be more socially intelligent, we become responsible historical actors who make constructive changes in destructive cultures. When we are aware of complex social realities, as well as committed to creating constructive cultures, we build the best societies or civilizations possible for the present and future.

In considering the nature of human nature, cultures as civilizations, and the power and complexities of cultures, social intelligence helps us to see that cultures are never static, but rather constantly change at different rates and in different ways. Even though we are inevitably caught up in societies' evolutionary needs to survive, we have choices in how we accomplish this. For example, we may try to create the best civilizations possible, or we may take no thought for the future, which often leads us to gradually self-destruct as individuals, communities, and societies.

When we become responsible historical actors, we aim to perpetuate our most constructive values, so that our future worlds are progressive and humane. Because cultures inevitably grow and diversify, we embrace these changes for our socially intelligent creative and innovative purposes, so that we both survive and prosper.

Diversification

As cultures grow and change, they predictably become more diverse. Ideally we are enriched by the cultural components of social diversity, but all too often cultures, groups, and individuals are challenged and even threatened by cultural contrasts. Because we easily become settled in our ways—another significant aspect of the nature of human nature—we take comfort in social stability or social security, and tend to block cultural changes that question our cultural and social assumptions. For example, we may resist well-intentioned social reforms merely because they emphasize the importance of accepting social diversity. Furthermore, even though we may understand that such reforms are in our long term interests, we prefer to maintain easy lifestyles, familiar ideas, and mistaken assumptions about our needs.

Because social intelligence is made up of practical strategies based on social facts, we can deepen our understanding of the extent to which increased social diversity is a fact of our social lives in contemporary societies. For example, we cannot turn back the tides of cultural diversification, so social intelligence helps us to accept and benefit from the inevitability of cultural diversity. At the same time that we see the richness of wide ranges of human and cultural expressions, we realize that acknowledging and embracing a diverse world can be our preferred option for enlightenment and fulfillment. Rather than resist diversity in our cultures, we benefit from welcoming and embracing diversity, so that we gain directly from the life-enhancing advantages of cultural varieties.

Social intelligence shows us that particular kinds of cultural and social diversity have more productive consequences than others. For example, social class opportunities to survive and prosper cannot build cultures and societies which are just and fair. Whenever and wherever social privileges are given to the few, many social disadvantages are shared by members of lower social classes. Elitist forms of contrived social differences do not benefit whole cultures and whole societies, because the self interests of a few dominate the common good, leaving many individual and social needs unmet.

By contrast, when our cultures are based on valuing all members of our populations, we form more solid foundations for perpetuating societies that are strong and balanced. We no longer compete endlessly for limited social rewards, for example, but rather use our talents to build more cooperative and more resilient cultures and societies, so that whole populations are fulfilled by contributing to the common good.

When our populations diversify, our cultures diversify. Our roles as historical actors include scrutinizing social and cultural differences, so that opportunities to be productive can be more widely shared, rather than restricted to a few. For example, social intelligence shows us ways to increase education, so that what historically were upper class social privileges are now available to others. In these respects cultures based on different races, ethnicities, genders, sexual orientations, ablebodiedness, and educations are accepted and valued by whole societies rather than used as ways to divide populations, privileges, and opportunities.

Practical socially intelligent approaches to accepting diversification in modern societies include increasing means for mass education, as well as changing traditional social class structures and privileges. When we realize the importance of educating all members of our societies to high standards, for example, we reduce the cultural and social risks involved in educating only the privileged few. Similarly, when we formulate and implement laws which protect all members of populations, we protect everyone's well-being. These avenues of social reform are widely accepted in Western societies, and are sometimes used as outreach strategies to countries which historically were exploited in the development of increasingly competitive global economies.

Perhaps less understood, as well as less accepted, are socially intelligent means of cultural change that increase our awareness of the advantages of social diversity, as well as our alertness to the negative and harmful consequences of not accepting and embracing social diversity. For example, a critical mass in our populations needs to realize that our only viable choice is to embrace social diversity, so that we can make substantial changes in our cultures.

Embracing social diversity must be our goal because we predictably perpetuate destructive cultures and societies when we sustain limited educational opportunities or vested interests in upper social class privileges. Unproductive but time-honored structures of social inequalities, which persist in many contemporary societies, must change through deliberately aiming for social diversity if our widely shared dreams of success and fulfillment are to be realized.

Barbaric or Refined Cultures?

Individuals, families, communities, and societies choose the cultures they create to establish particular supports and directions for their everyday lives, survival, and fulfillment. Cultures are ongoing works in progress and we reinforce or challenge existing cultures, as well as innovate by bringing about new cultures, when we make our daily decisions as individuals, families, communities, and societies.

Cultures range between many different extremes, which depend largely on the basic values expressed by cultures. For example, we can think of cultures as being constructive or destructive, competitive or cooperative, life-enhancing or restrictive, violent or peaceful, and barbaric or refined. Although the ranges of variations in cultures between these polar opposites are infinite, distinctive patterns in the values of different cultures guide our assessments of whether we want to accept or change the values of existing cultures.

Social intelligence helps us to discern the fact that our overall comparisons of cultures and cultural values depend largely on whether our cultures restrict human possibilities, or nurture the development of the human potentials of individuals, families, communities, and societies. Social intelligence also teaches us that we are responsible for creating and sustaining the cultural and social conditions of our particular situations, and that we have choices in how we bring particular values into being as we express our dependencies on others.

We often believe that our day-to-day lives are easier if we do not pay attention to our choices to construct preferred cultures in our communications and transactions with others. However, social intelligence shows us that we cannot afford the costs related to ignoring the power and complexities of the social influences of families, beliefs, social classes, cultures, and societies. Unless we gain sufficient understanding of these five major social influences in our lives, and their impacts on how we behave, our situations become unmanageable, and we inevitably create selves, families, communities, and societies that we would prefer not to have.

When we conduct ourselves without deliberate thought, and make decisions which we experience as "natural" or spontaneous, we tend to maintain the status quo, which is usually dominated by special interests or social conditions that facilitate the materialistic gains of members of upper social classes. However, when we understand our lives in relation to our cultures and value choices, we can choose to make real differences in our cultural and social situations. For example, we gradually realize that we create more constructive possibilities for cultural changes when we respond directly to—rather than ignore—these existential challenges.

Social intelligence shows us that recognizing historical facts in the wide ranges of cultures within and among societies, gives us solid bases for understanding the power and complexities of cultural and social influences. We use our informed social awareness to scrutinize our decisions and commitments, for example, so that we can take more inspired actions. If we decide to change some of the destructive or barbaric aspects of our contemporary cultures, we must orient our actions according to social ideals and values that encourage individual and social expressions of constructive values. We are more predisposed to being altruistic, or to developing individual and social potentials, when we act according to cultural values and ideals which reinforce these priorities.

Social intelligence suggests that refined cultures derive from establishing cultural and social conditions that increase equality, inclusiveness, diversity, cooperation, and openness among individuals, families, communities, and societies. We need to see, realize, and understand complex nuances in the power of cultural and social influences, for example, in order to enlighten our decision-making, so that we are more socially astute in making commitments to cultural and social ideals. When we increase our social intelligence, we move in directions which enhance life rather than restrict it, and we gradually increase the common good and social justice of refined cultures.

History shows us that we have made some progress in recognizing the rights of individuals and groups that were exploited, oppressed, or discriminated against in the past. Social intelligence encourages us to take these social facts into account as evidence that significant social changes can be made to increase positive qualities in our social situations, as well as strengthen our capacities to meet the needs of dependent individuals and groups in our societies. Our awareness as socially intelligent historical actors makes achieving these goals possible, because we create socially intelligent strategies to change our cultures constructively.

Now and Always
"Now" and "always" draw our attention to the time dimensions of cultures as civilizations. However, when we consider past, present, and future cultures as civilizations, we need pointers to anchor particular aspects of our cultures and civilizations, so that we are not overwhelmed by their power and complexities. For example, we use social intelligence to

guide our understanding of cultures and civilizations in the past, present, and future, or to trace particular aspects of changing cultures within civilizations.

Social intelligence shows us that if we want to change our cultures in order to change our civilizations, we must act in timely ways, as well as to consider the vital time perspectives of pasts, present, and futures. However, even though social intelligence directs us to pay close attention to the past histories of our ongoing social situations, we mostly need to use past facts to understand the present. This emphasis ensures that we take more thoughtful actions in the present, which create the futures that we truly want.

In examining past cultures, we begin by finding patterns in social facts which show us that much human suffering results from widespread lacks in education, for example. These destructive cultures and their harmful social consequences lead us to make more informed decisions about how to create cultures today that avoid similar problems, and ensure more constructive futures for whole populations and civilizations.

Other approaches to understanding past, present, and future cultures and civilizations include looking at the parts that the major social influences of families, beliefs, social classes, and societies play in our past, present, and future cultures. For example, many communities and societies have cultures that are largely fuelled by families' values, motivations, and actions. Emotional investments in particular ideals and values, especially when selected and transmitted through several generations of families, become dynamic cultural forces, and make significant differences in cultural and social outcomes in the present and future.

Similarly, beliefs—often originating in our families— generate world views and social ideals which orient individual and collective actions in the present for the future. Making sense of our worlds, which is what our beliefs accomplish, is an important social influence. Our beliefs and their related values are instrumental in establishing our priorities, because they determine how we choose particular social ideals, values, and courses of action in our everyday lives in the present for the future.

Although the restrictiveness of social class influences for many individuals and groups in the past, and continuing in the present, may not inspire clear choices for improved futures, linking social classes to cultures is a meaningful way to become more socially intelligent, and to assess our responsibilities as historical actors. For example, changing social class cultures often changes social classes. Furthermore, we create new cultures for the future whenever we change present injustices in social classes.

Social intelligence shows us that globalization—particularly through the global economy—has significant impacts on societies' cultures. For example, our cultures are influenced by both the societies in which we live and relationships among societies in the international community and world markets. Social intelligence helps us to assess contrasts in the power of cultures in the world arena, and shows us that we must work toward discovering—and incorporating—more universalistic values to protect our cultures from the economic dominance of capitalism, or from politically powerful societies. There is much work to be done to create viable global cultures, so that constructive civilizations survive and thrive in the present and future.

Even though we cannot make decisions in the present which guarantee our futures—we cannot control the infinite dimensions of our social realities—we can persist in our efforts to establish social ideals that we believe in the most, and act as if we are deciding our futures now. Existential imperatives suggest that responsible actions are based on views of the past, present, and future. Consequently, acting as though we impact individuals, families, communities, societies, and civilizations after we are dead can be meaningful motives to create the best of all possible futures now. Our actions need to transcend our immediate social situations if we are to be socially intelligent in our survival and fulfillment for the long run.

I. Cultures as Civilizations

New Cultures, New Values

One of the primary characteristics of our cultures is that they are the omnipresent underpinnings of all societies in all places and at all times. Cultures are the lifeblood of civilizations, in that human beings need to use symbols and meanings in order to build and use knowledge, as well as to establish humane modes of being as individuals, families, communities, and societies.

Social intelligence honors these connections among peoples and societies by expanding the knowledge base of civilizations. For example, social intelligence uses social facts to understand essential choices and strategies that human beings employ in their interactions and communications with each other. Furthermore, social intelligence shows us that we survive and are fulfilled because we develop reasons or purposes to live, as well as goals to accomplish as individuals, societies, and civilizations.

In these broad and deep respects, social intelligence helps us to be objective about subjective aspects of our lives which are intrinsically difficult to manage, and which could lead to individual and social destruction or extinction. For example, social intelligence helps us to take charge of our emotional inclinations to be thoughtlessly reactive toward others, by examining our investments in values, special interests, or destructive ways of interacting. This frees us to make socially intelligent commitments to create new civilizations or new worlds, by building new cultures from new values.

Giving new emphases to already established historical values, like equality, may reinforce or challenge existing cultures. We make commitments to increase our social intelligence, for example, so that we are more discriminating in making value choices, and more effective in accomplishing our preferred goals, the common good, and social justice.

Although there are many different interpretations of social justice, we can unite in taking collective action to accomplish some of the shared goals of social justice, such as decreasing the suffering of those who cannot help themselves in our societies. When we become more socially intelligent, we realize that we have ethical and moral responsibilities to meet the needs of others, rather than make the machinery of unregulated capitalism more powerful.

One of the advanced stages of increasing our social intelligence is that we act from bases of social facts. For example, we become more aware of the cultural and social consequences of historical changes, so that we deliberately develop more constructive cultures which express new or relatively ignored life-enhancing values. The most significant innovations and achievements of civilizations often derive from new values and new cultures, with the result that our refined cultural achievements become more consistent and enduring.

For example, when we consider the relatively recent changes in gender and sexual orientation in Western civilizations, we see how new ways of valuing gender and differences in sexual orientations shift traditional modes of being in these societies. We make new kinds of freedom and equality possible by valuing genders and sexual orientations more equally, so that the social consequences of these changes in our cultures create breakthroughs for members of younger generations and future generations.

Social intelligence shows us that such shifts in cultures and values are consistent with historical social realities—especially where individual and collective rights and responsibilities have increased. For example, we continue to move in constructive directions when we choose to take charge of our individual and collective decision-making in our everyday behavior.

We do not have to be political leaders of nation states in order to make important cultural and social contributions. Rather, social intelligence shows us that we need to exercise our individual and collective rights or responsibilities to enhance our shared well-being and fulfillment. For example, we strengthen civilizations through our value choices, as well as through goal-directed efforts to build new cultures.

I. Cultures as Civilizations

However powerful and complex our cultures are, we inevitably express the dignity of our human nature when we make personal and collective commitments to improve specific qualities of life in our civilizations. Because we have already changed many ways in which we parent and educate our children, we can now attend to changing other barriers to civilized living. For example, undoing racial prejudice and discrimination must be a high priority in building new cultures from new values. Social intelligence offers us real hope in these difficult endeavors because the knowledge base of social intelligence is built on social facts, predictabilities, and the importance of optimizing our possibilities for the future.

II. Local and Global Cultures

When we look at the scope of our cultures, we are easily overwhelmed by their extensive breadth and depth. These are powers that are beyond our lived experiences, and it is awesome to even imagine that we have any control over our cultural and social destinies. However, social intelligence encourages us to learn about the cultural and social dimensions of our cultures, so that we are more likely to use cultures for beneficial purposes in our civilizations today for tomorrow.

Cultures permeate the depths of our individual being, as well as the farthest reaches of our societies. However, because cultures are human products, they are necessarily limited by shared beliefs about human civilizations, human potential, and human development. Nevertheless, in spite of these intrinsic restrictions on the power and complexities of cultures—for example, cultures are not integral parts of unexplored and unsettled parts of our world—cultures maintain considerable power over individuals' and societies' destinies and well-being.

Cultures are particularly powerful and complex, because they have overlapping impacts on qualities of our lives, especially in terms of their local and global connectedness. Although our cultures are necessarily rooted in particular historical and geographical realities, they are also connected to the furthest points of our human and social universes. In addition, human beings are carriers of cultures. For example, explorers who traveled to previously unexplored and unsettled territories inevitably brought with them their own cultural ways of perceiving and dealing with their discoveries.

To the extent that people are born into cultures, they are connected to global cultures whether they realize it or not, and whether they pay attention to the consequences of this social fact or not. We are products of both local and global cultural influences because we are human beings. Social intelligence enriches our awareness about these necessary cultural connections, so that we become more deliberate historical actors within the power, complexities, and challenges of our cultures.

The particular importance of local cultures, in contrast to global cultures, is that we more easily develop a deep understanding of what our value choices are in local cultures. For example, we often recognize fairly quickly that our families have established ways of doing things that differ from other families' habits. Consequently, we heighten our senses of cultural uniqueness through our family experiences and family observations. Furthermore, when we have kin members who live in different countries, or who have contrasting family histories, we more easily appreciate the rootedness of our original local cultures, as well as the power of global cultures to redefine family dependencies in our local cultures.

Social intelligence suggests that we can usefully explore some of the impacts of local and global cultures through examining contrasts in major social influences such as families, beliefs, social classes, cultures, and societies. When we see how cultures underlie or direct these social influences through the past, present, and future, we more objectively assess their impacts on our decision-making and actions as individuals and societies. For example, when we see the local and global cultural dimensions of social justice, we identify future goals and possibilities for ourselves and others in relation to the social problems and social issues of our current situations.

In assessing the power and complexities of local and global cultures, we see the choices we have to understand these connections by focusing on a specific value such as equality. Valuing social intelligence in its own right also gives us a secure starting point for taking more control over our cultures. Social intelligence guides us to make wiser choices of values and other cultural means, so that we influence our lives and shared destinies more directly.

Social intelligence reminds us that knowledge brings responsibilities, and that the tasks of changing cultures and civilizations are difficult but rewarding. When the going gets rough as we move in these directions, we need to turn in directions which change our values and cultures. Consequently, sooner or later, we experience tangible rewards from making cultural shifts in our priorities.

Rootedness in the Present

Social intelligence and historical evidence show that local and global cultures have always been interconnected, and will continue to be so in the future. However isolated individuals and groups may appear to be in our communities and societies, we are ultimately linked to each other through our social and physical environments. We also realize, from recently developed ecological perspectives, how social and physical contexts of our survival and fulfillment define both limits and achievements in our local and global cultures.

When we scrutinize the social roots of our local and global cultures, we find historical facts that describe how early groups promoted cultural patterns of settlement and interaction, as well as established traditional ways of being and acting. These are beginnings and foundations of our cultures and civilizations, because unless communities settled at the same time that they met their basic needs to survive, repetitions in cultural exchanges were not reinforced through intergenerational exchanges.

Social intelligence helps us to recognize the importance and significance of our historical origins, so that we identify more deeply with local and global cultural heritages such as social rituals and social institutions. Furthermore, because of the immediacy of our current needs and the demands of our particular social situations, we benefit from understanding how our local and global cultures are connected, and how our local and global cultures influence our decisions, priorities, and world views. For example, we are not free agents until we manage to unsnarl—and come to terms with—some of the power and complexities of local and global cultural influences on our ideals, ideas, goals, assessments of the past, awareness of the present, and visions for the future.

Cultural interpretations of social realities often privilege historical sources as vital ways to understand our rootedness in social conditions. Social intelligence adds significant breadth and social dimensions to established cultural and historical views of who we are. For example, because of the power and complexities of social systems and the social influences of families, beliefs, social classes, cultures, and societies, social intelligence suggests that we need to give priority to the social fact that our current living conditions are enmeshed in both local and global cultures. Although we often experience our values as originating in our families, our local and global cultures are sources that families use to select their most meaningful values. We also learn, in our families, how to express our families' values through our local and global cultures.

The ways in which our local cultures interact with our global cultures depend on how much influence and power our local cultures have in relation to global cultures. For example, when our local cultures contrast starkly with global cultures, our local cultures may be viewed as exotically different by others, rather than as having widespread social status or social significance. When our local cultures are similar to global cultures—such as the local cultures found in cosmopolitan global cities in modern industrialized societies—our local cultures may be defined as being forward looking, trend setting, or centers of power.

Whatever associations we make with respect to our local and global cultures, social intelligence requires that we discover and understand some of the powerful and complex cultural differences and similarities that influence our lives and their outcomes. When we are more objective about the significance of cultural values in establishing our most basic survival or fulfillment priorities, for example, we gain control over our cultural choices, decision-making, and commitments. This heightened cultural awareness is a significant precondition for becoming socially intelligent historical actors, who meet family responsibilities and at the same time increase social justice.

The most effective way to honor connections between our local and global cultures is to remain rooted in the present. For example, we assess and understand the constantly changing facts of our current circumstances in as many of their local and global cultural contexts as possible. We formulate our priorities, decisions, and commitments according to our rootedness in present local and global cultural realities, at the same time that we use history to inform our present and futures. Knowledge of our local and global cultural starting points, which results from our efforts to become more socially intelligent, enhances our effectiveness in accomplishing individual and collective goals to improve the common good and increase social justice.

Local and Global Families

Social intelligence views our families as ongoing sources of our attitudes to life, as well as ongoing sources of our societies. Because of the critical functions of families, and because of the emotional intensity of family dependencies, understanding families—and their local and global connections—is a foundation of our social intelligence.

Furthermore, when we examine local and global cultures from socially intelligent perspectives, we need to consider the influences of families, beliefs, social classes, and societies in local and global cultures. We need to see, for example, that whatever goes on in our families is significant for local and global cultures, partly because our beliefs and social classes originate and are perpetuated in our families' cultures.

We learn important differences between right and wrong in our families during our earliest years. Moral contrasts are also at the core of local and global cultures, because without some agreement on basic definitions of right and wrong, our communities and societies could not exist or thrive. Moral imperatives fuel and inspire our choices of social ideals, and families reinforce or negatively sanction our morals and social ideals. Our families continue to have powerful influences over us, especially because we grew through intense family dependencies when we were young. Therefore, social intelligence encourages us to change problematic aspects of our family relationships, in order to gain control over our moral decisions and commitments.

Benefits from changing our interactions with our families, in relation to our values and ideals, may transform our lives. Local and global cultural awareness necessarily leads us to compare our own families with other families, for example, so that we become more objective about how we were oriented to ourselves and the world through our families' exchanges. Our value choices are particularly important—as children or adults—because establishing our own priorities defines our life tasks, as well as our successes in accomplishing our goals.

Because our starting points in understanding our families necessarily focus on local cultures, we need to see how our families relate to our communities, as well as to what extent they provide leadership—or follow others—with regard to moral concerns. Lifestyle aspects of everyday value choices are also important in understanding the impacts of family and community cultures on our early development as individuals.

Our broader awareness of national and international cultural influences often develops from our families' contacts with religious congregations, or from being students in elementary schools. For example, outsiders' family cultures may be stark contrasts to our own family cultures. Moreover, at the same time that our social contacts multiply throughout our development as adults, we become increasingly aware of wider ranges of cultural choices that individuals and families make in accomplishing their life tasks.

Social intelligence draws our attention to the fact that it is important to recognize and expand this progression in cultural awareness whenever possible. For example, social intelligence helps us to realize that we see our worlds differently when we deliberately emphasize particular values as priorities, and that our beliefs influence who we are in relation to our families, communities, and societies.

Family cultures give us specific views of cultures, because families have needs and tasks to perform in order to survive and maintain themselves. Furthermore, understanding global trends in family behavior shows us how different approaches in everyday life influence our capacities to increase or decrease our social intelligence and productivity. A case can be made that we are cultural beings at our core, and that our value choices establish our identities, as well as our most significant social and cultural commitments.

Local and global family cultures also orient us to time. Although many families do not honor their ancestors, all families benefit from compiling family histories that show how their families coped with crises during recent generations. For example, we gain strength to pursue particular dreams and ideals through examining our families in the past, because our present and future orientations are more informed about possibilities for change and varied outcomes.

Families show us how to survive, how to fight with each other productively, how to cooperate, and how to compete. We tend to feel secure in our local family cultures, for example, because then we know that whatever we do our families will usually not shun us. Understanding other families—in both local and global contexts—helps us to see how strong patterns of interdependence support all family members.

Families not only teach us about cultures when we are young, but also show us a great deal about value choices today. For example, we look at wide contrasts among families to show us more clearly how we and others habitually relate to each other, and what our preferred modes of being are. Furthermore, patterns in family interactions tend to be more predictable than individual or group behavior in other social settings. This predictability allows us to continue to assess our current local and global family cultures more accurately, as well as their influences on our actions.

Local and Global Beliefs

In addition to family, social class, and societal dimensions of local and global cultures, social intelligence suggests that beliefs are important influences in our cultures. Beliefs are often more critical influences in our cultures than families, social classes, and societies, because they are central and essential components of cultures.

Social intelligence singles out beliefs as having independent, powerful influences in cultures because of their emotional intensity, especially in relation to clusters of values within particular beliefs such as beliefs about religions or politics. Beliefs give emotional charges to values, ideas, ideals, expectations, knowledge, religions, and legal systems.

Beliefs also derive from families, social classes, cultures, and societies. In spite of the omnipresence of beliefs and the assumptions we make in defining ourselves and our social worlds, some beliefs are more powerful than others—largely our most deep-seated beliefs that have been passed down from generation to generation in our families.

As we consider the relative influences of both local and global beliefs in our cultures, we necessarily draw on our own experiences of beliefs. For example, we may recall that local beliefs seemed more powerful in our development as children, while global beliefs were often experienced as more influential in our adult lives.

Depending on our different patterns of travel or migration, people who choose to reside in countries other than where they were born may progressively heighten their cosmopolitan, global awareness by absorbing new beliefs, or may constantly yearn to return to the geographical milieus of their original local beliefs. Thus, although our geographical locations do not determine what our beliefs are, they often prompt us to adapt to our original local beliefs in particular ways.

II. Local and Global Cultures

Individuals who spend their whole lives in one geographical area do not necessarily maintain their original local beliefs. For example, education and mass media often open up global realities and global beliefs to audiences in all social and geographical settings. However, even when several of our most important original local beliefs are modified by education and mass media, we may retain the emotional intensity and meaningful significance of particular local beliefs, such as our religions. Also, when we modify some of our local beliefs, so that they become global beliefs, we do not necessarily change all our beliefs.

Whatever the balance, or shifting balance, of individuals' or groups' local and global beliefs, we need to examine both local and global beliefs in order to understand their roles in our cultures and in our lives. One of the particular characteristics of beliefs to note, whether they are local or global beliefs, is that they often resist change, even though individuals or groups may have experienced many years of formal education. For example, students who attend world renowned universities often compartmentalize their lives, so that they may intellectually embrace social ideals such as freedom, but at the same time live out multiple local social class beliefs which severely limit the freedom of members of lower social classes.

In these respects, our vested interests in our own well-being—which are often our strongest beliefs—frequently override our less strong beliefs and commitments, which may include universal values such as freedom for all. Furthermore, unless we see these discrepancies or contradictions in our beliefs, as well as wholeheartedly want to change them, our vested interests will continue to override our other individual and social beliefs.

Vested interests, which everyone has, are expressed in beliefs that permeate all aspects of our being, and have important consequences for our local and global cultures. We are more likely to temper the impacts of beliefs related to our vested interests, however, when we see connections and contradictions in our beliefs, and aspire to new goals such as increasing social intelligence or social justice. For example, social intelligence guides our efforts to substitute constructive beliefs for destructive or harmful vested interest beliefs, so that we change patterns of interactions in our families or other social settings.

One of the most powerful single beliefs we have may be our belief in the salience of our religions. When we are observant worshippers in our religions, we routinely make commitments to related beliefs and values, which are often associated with divine sanctions. Fearing the wrath of God, for example, may reinforce and deepen our religious beliefs, which makes it more difficult to change or modify them. These social influences affect our lives deeply because we accept clusters of values in our religious beliefs. Consequently, our religious beliefs may define both our local and global cultures, and govern how we think we are expected to act in our families and other social settings.

Social intelligence requires us to examine all our beliefs, so that we determine more objectively the extent to which we continue to cherish or change our beliefs. Social intelligence also encourages us to assess our beliefs in light of local and global cultures that substantiate or challenge our beliefs, and in light of local and global cultural ideals of social justice. These assessments help us to make more informed decisions about which cultural beliefs to keep, and which to replace with more life-enhancing or more realistic cultural beliefs.

Local and Global Social Classes

Many of us know, sometimes as children, that social class cultures were first communicated to us in our families and local community settings. However, only when we have a fairly sophisticated understanding of the complexities and power of social classes and social class cultures, do we realize the extent to which local and global social class cultures influence our day-to-day lives. Although local social class cultures may motivate us to be productive at local and national levels, global social class cultures often call into question the adequacy and realities of our original—perhaps naïve—local social class cultures.

Social intelligence shows us that we need to asses the significance of both our local and global social class cultures in relation to families, beliefs, social classes, cultures, and societies. Only when we see complex overlapping social influences in our local and global social class cultures, are we able to change our local and global social class cultures. The breadth of social intelligence perspectives gradually changes possibilities and realities, by guiding us to assess and interact differently in our local and global social class cultures.

The dominance of social class cultures is often expressed most clearly at local levels. We experience our families and communities largely through the prisms and restrictiveness of local social class cultures, for example, so that we necessarily learn how to be and how to act in relation to local social class cultural standards rather than broad social concerns.

When we realize the pervasiveness of local social class cultural influences on how we think and what we do, we begin to change their impacts. Nevertheless, for many of us, the power and complexities of social class cultures are such that we often do not easily recognize the cultural or social class sources of these restrictive influences, so that we conduct ourselves as though it is "natural" or "required" for us to accept and conform to social class cultures.

For example, we may have been encouraged to make particular friends when we were young, preferences which flowed from our parents' social class cultures, so that even our likes and dislikes conformed to—or rebelled from—specific social class cultural preferences. Because we often continue to believe that we need social classes in order to survive or be fulfilled, we inadvertently perpetuate social classes and their underlying cultures.

When we are older, well-educated, or widely traveled, we may accept socially intelligent broad perspectives on social class cultures. For example, people from lower social classes are often painfully aware that upper social class cultures are different from middle and lower social class cultures, and that upper social class cultures reinforce social class hierarchies throughout societies. When we have this level of social awareness, we may decide to challenge rather than support mainstream social class cultures.

Social intelligence requires us to consider social class cultures which stretch beyond national boundaries. For example, we may identify social class cultures that underlie the global economy and support international divisions of labor. We find that global social class cultures reflect world religions, races, ethnicities, or shared cultural and political histories. Furthermore, particular levels of education often define global social class cultures along lines of contrasts in literacy, academic accomplishments, scientific discoveries, technologies, medical services, artistic achievements, musical styles, and mass media influences. Social class differences in successfully living our individual and collective dreams—such as "the American dream"—suggest that both local and global social class cultures uphold social inequalities by restricting opportunities.

People may challenge what is thought of as idyllic patterns in local social class cultures by reacting negatively to local cultures that uphold traditional social inequalities. For example, local and international migrations occur when the global economy standardizes both local and global cultures according to the vested interests of powerful multinational companies and international economic organizations.

Social intelligence encourages us to understand these cultural complexities, so that economic and political interests do not overwhelm our capacities to make thoughtful cultural choices each day. For example, we may choose to select our local cultural priorities more deliberately, or become more informed about global cultural decision-making and social class cultures. Our acts have lasting impacts on broad social trends, especially when we choose to increase the common good and social justice as goals, rather than merely conform to local or global social class cultures. Social intelligence makes us more responsible and more effective historical actors when we account for both local and global social class cultures in our decisions, actions, and aims.

Local and Global Societies

The broadest strands of culture, which must be considered in order to understand differences between local and global cultures, are societal cultures. Although in the past nation states were thought of as societal cultures in their own right, in recent times globalization has become a strong international cultural force that can no longer be ignored. Furthermore, due to the significance of the increasing momentum of global cultural changes, "local" may now relate to whole societies, while "global" refers to cultures of the international community in a single world society.

Thus local and global societies often play increasingly influential roles in local and global cultures. At the same time, mass media magnify and distort our knowledge of societal trends and cultural patterns. For example, local aspects of societies may be emphasized to increase a sense of belonging or community within particular societies. In times of political tensions, patriotism is increased deliberately through specific news presentations. Also, business corporations, advertising industries, or political parties frequently manipulate societal cultures to enhance our impressions that societies have distinctive cultures.

Mass media are strong community and societal influences. For example, we often learn what is most distinctive about our local communities and national societies through mass media. We also understand what globalization is through particular media presentations. For example, daily news footage opens up cultural contacts with the rest of the world, as well as enhances our awareness of other societies' cultures.

What we thought were cultural influences rather than political forces raises questions about relationships among power, social status, societies, and local or global cultures. For example, social intelligence helps us to understand the impacts of social classes and societies on local and global cultures by delineating interdependencies in international power relations.

Families, beliefs, social classes, and societies have considerable impacts on local and global cultures. Modern societies show us that local and global cultures are not monolithic, even though historically local cultures were more homogeneous than global cultures. However, in spite of contrasts between cultures in countries at different levels of economic and political development, the world economy has encouraged materialistic world cultures. For example, products made by multinational corporations in different countries are increasingly available, including countries that are at contrasting stages of economic and political development.

We draw strength from socially intelligent views of cultures in societies, globalization, and civilizations. The values of different cultures reflect the power and complexities of both historical and contemporary cultures. Furthermore, even though social intelligence emphasizes the importance of being rooted in current social and cultural realities, we must use historical knowledge if we are to understand cultural contrasts in local and global societies. For example, history shows us that current global conflicts emerge from multigenerational tribalism as well as our oldest communities and societies.

Even though we may not want to associate patterns in cultures with patterns in economic and political power, these patterns exist and should not be ignored. Social intelligence helps us to be more objective about these social realities and social situations so that we face them squarely, rather than merely retreat from them or react.

We often want the world to be different because we believe that we cannot control problematic aspects of cultures and societies. However, social intelligence gives us means to adapt more successfully to irresoluble conflicts of interest. For example, we become more aware historical actors who use current cultural resources for constructive rather than destructive purposes, if being socially intelligent in our actions is a high priority.

Considering the power and complexities of cultures in local and global societies allows us to gain some control over our decisions, commitments, actions, and social ideals. Our choices range from designing strategic purposeful adaptations to historical trends, to actively resisting or initiating historical trends. For example, social intelligence helps us to resist societal dimensions of cultures when we scrutinize and change our habits of purchasing goods and services, or when we act expressly to break away from some of the cultural conditions and consequences of capitalism. We become freer agents when we increase our social intelligence to become historical actors, because then we do whatever we can to establish social justice—as individuals, communities, and societies.

Social Justice in Cultures

Our consideration of the parts that families, beliefs, social classes, and societies play in understanding local and global cultures heightens our awareness of the power and complexities of cultures. Social intelligence shows us that it is vitally important to continue to learn about the many facets of our cultures in order to live fully, make sound decisions, and take enlightened actions. We cannot afford to ignore the independent and dependent powers of cultures, because our lives would not truly be our own.

Both local and global cultures provide us with values, beliefs, ideas, ideals, and goals. When we are socially intelligent we are aware of the power and complexities of social and cultural influences, we act after considering these influences carefully, and we modify them to increase social justice. Whereas social intelligence is merely a means to an end, choosing which goals to pursue is an ethical, existential concern. When we are socially intelligent, we see that we cannot survive and live fully unless the human rights of all are respected, and conditions for the freedom of all are established.

Social justice is one of the end points or goals of becoming socially intelligent. When we recognize the constructive dimensions of our social situations more clearly through social intelligence, we find that meeting the ongoing needs of ourselves and our families is not necessarily a sufficient contribution to the common good. We benefit more from sustaining some idealistic quests, such as social justice, so that we meet basic community or societal needs, as well as our own needs and those of our families.

Social justice is supported and reinforced by particular values—such as equality, inclusiveness, diversity, cooperation, and openness—and their related beliefs, which are rooted in our local and global cultures. In some respects both social intelligence and social justice are means to bring about cultural changes that would not otherwise happen. For example, when we describe our interests in terms of social justice, we are more likely to find like-minded others who want to pursue similar cultural goals.

We experience both social justice and social injustices through the cultures and social conditions of our families, beliefs, social classes, and societies. When we concentrate on the values and beliefs of social justice, we see more clearly which values and beliefs we need to choose and strengthen, in order to become more socially intelligent and increase social justice. Consequently, when we act deliberately to achieve social justice, we become more socially intelligent and contribute to the common good.

The common good is a cultural ideal which expresses values such as equality and cooperation. Contributing to the common good is an essential aspect of being socially intelligent, because when we increase our social intelligence our efforts to meet others' needs are more effective. Social intelligence is a capacity and resource we are born with, in order to survive and thrive as children. However, when we are adults, we need to deliberately increase our social intelligence in order to be more responsible, so that we find more workable solutions for problematic social issues.

II. Local and Global Cultures

Just as we can identify cultural aspects of our families, beliefs, social classes, and societies, we can find cultural dimensions of social justice in our families, beliefs, social classes, and societies. Sometimes, however, we may become overwhelmed by the choices we could make to increase social justice, especially when our own family members are needy.

Existentially, we are forced to make value choices about our priorities—an under-rated but vital process in putting our lives in order—so we need to be aware of the particular values or beliefs we want to realize through our actions. For example, we might consider teaching less privileged students to be very important, but at the same time need the security of a reasonably high income to meet our families' needs. This dilemma requires that we decide whether it is more important for us to teach less privileged people than to earn a high income in a less socially rewarding job. Thus, our contributions to the common good vary according to the priorities we establish in our cultural value choices.

One of the strengths of the ideals of social justice is that social justice is interpreted in many different ways. For example, we need to create means that motivate us to make sound contributions to the common good, so that we continue to be aware individuals through increasing our social intelligence. We often do not become socially intelligent merely because we want to be socially intelligent, but rather because we want to make the world a better place. We do not aim to get along with others well when we aspire to be more socially intelligent, but rather find ways to make commitments with others to accomplish difficult tasks like bringing new social justice values into being.

Social justice cultural values are reflected in both local and global cultures. For example, we choose local cultural contexts of social justice to express our social intelligence and historical concerns in the initial stages of increasing our social intelligence. However, when we develop a more mature social intelligence, social intelligence principles guide us in understanding global dimensions of social justice by being responsible historical or international actors.

At best, historical actors use social intelligence to coordinate and integrate both local and global cultural social justice concerns, so that they make effective cultural innovations. Ultimately, global cultures are often more of a focus for historical actors than local cultures. For example, the broadest social justice cultural changes are often in the global scope of historical actors' collective actions. Thus, syntheses of local and global cultures guide historical actors' thinking, and are expressed through global actions to increase social justice.

III. Cultures Cause Changes?

It is neat and tidy to think that cultures cause social changes, and that we can bring about changes by manipulating our cultures. However, social processes are more complex than this. We need to consider which social realities are involved in bringing about changes, before we can realistically assess whether or not to design and pursue goals of cultural innovations in our own lives, communities, and societies.

Because no single cause brings about social changes, understanding the interaction of complex social processes leads to fruitful explanations of how cultures "cause" changes. To some extent social intelligence shows us that cultures are instrumental in influencing social changes, especially when we account for the power and complexities of cultures in our lives as individuals, communities, and societies. For example, our changing cultures precipitate particular kinds of social changes, even though they alone do not cause social changes.

Social intelligence encourages us to take broad views of how cultures interact with societies, and how these exchanges impact qualities of our lives. A well-established, credible way to gain this understanding is to examine historical trends, and to collect significant social facts. For example, it is largely through the passage of time that cultural and social changes are recorded, so that we can now identify more clearly some of the most characteristic patterns of cultural and social changes in the lives of individuals, communities, and societies.

Social intelligence also keeps us rooted in the present, in order to understand the power and complexities of cultures and other social influences today. For example, when we observe how people live in contemporary societies, we are often struck by the ongoing transforming impacts of consumer behavior. Acquiring material goods has gradually changed our cultural values and lifestyles, and conspicuous consumption has become a goal for members of most social classes. Consequently, some contemporary social class differences are blurred in important respects, but at the same time consumer behaviors still reveal extreme contrasts between the purchasing power and cultural habits of members of upper and lower social classes.

Seeing the industrial revolution as both a result of cultural changes and a cause of cultural changes helps us to recognize that cultural trends are significant aspects of market economies and social changes. For example, we begin to recognize how social traditions and religions have gradually lost their hold over cultures, which may yield different social consequences for entire populations in globalization.

Societies have become increasingly secular during industrialization, with the result that science and technology influence our individual and social identities, as well as our cultures. For example, we now value the results, and often the means, which science and technology provide in modern societies—values which gradually modify or replace traditional and religious values.

Because of these dramatic cultural and economic changes, we need to question whether we want to keep our worlds the way they are becoming, or whether we prefer to challenge these complex changes by gaining some control over them through deliberately designed strategies and goals of innovative cultural changes. For example, if we act collectively with people who share the ideal of social justice, we can have significant impacts on the cultural values that we really cherish in our personal lives, communities, and societies.

One of the primary purposes of understanding the power and complexities of cultures in the midst of broad social changes is to discover how we can make constructive differences in cultures' impacts on societies. For example, when we consider how religions and values have influenced social changes or the industrial revolution, we realize that having new compelling world views impacts widespread behavior patterns, capacities to cooperate to achieve collective goals, and abilities to create viable cultural innovations for our futures.

Social intelligence suggests that these are worthwhile activities, which may turn cultures toward supporting viable civilizations rather than unjust social conditions. The knowledge base of social intelligence gives us more options to accept or reject our current cultures, so that we can find strategic ways to make cultural innovations. Furthermore, when we commit ourselves to increasing our social intelligence, we become more effective historical actors, as well as more enlightened in our efforts to strengthen social justice with like-minded others.

Cause-Effect as Process

Social intelligence makes us aware of the power and complexities of social influences, such as cultures, that restrict or inspire our choices, decisions, and actions. Social intelligence can also be thought of in broad terms such as the sum total of how populations, societies, and civilizations think, establish their priorities, and act in relation to globalization. In these respects social intelligence is a body of knowledge that we create from historical and contemporary social facts, which allows us to be more objective and more enlightened in making significant social assessments and judgments, such as how to utilize our resources or how to educate the next generations.

Social intelligence suggests that when we focus on cultures, and on how cultures control our lives individually and collectively, we see that cultures are produced by many social influences as well as impact social influences. Social intelligence requires that we use this kind of social systems thinking to guide our interpretations and analyses of cultures, so that we become more astute and aware in our understanding of the power and complexities of the cultures that we express through our actions. Furthermore, social intelligence emphasizes that it is only with considerable social awareness that we can be effective in increasing the common good and social justice.

From the point of view of social intelligence, culture is one of five major social influences that have powerful effects on our capacities to accomplish our preferred goals. These five social influences—families, beliefs, social classes, cultures, and societies—largely define our emotional orientations to others, as well as our world views. Consequently, we choose either to succumb to these influences, or take control over some of their power though our decisions and commitments.

We benefit from looking closely at the five major social influences and their impacts on our cultures. This deepens our understanding of how social and cultural systems define and determine our destinies, unless we deliberately develop and use socially intelligent strategies to protect and preserve our freedom and autonomy.

For example, although families do not simply cause who we are, they play critical roles in how we think and what we do, especially with regard to how we understand and act according to our cultural resources. Because families select values from societies' cultures for their family cultures, we are raised to emphasize specific values more than others. This complex mix of cultural and social influences goes beyond simple cause-effect explanations. Rather, we are who we are, as family members, because of how our cultures, family dynamics, family dependencies, beliefs, and social class circumstances overlap and interact.

Similarly, although many of our beliefs—especially our religious beliefs—originated in our societies' and families' cultures, we are not solely cultural products of how our beliefs were developed and practiced. However, we need to understand and be vigilant about our families' dependencies, patterns in our families' leadership, their social class beliefs, and ways in which we were educated, for example, before we can understand cultural processes in the broad social contexts of our beliefs and behaviors.

Social classes, another major social influence, permeate our cultures, family cultures, and beliefs. We often survive as families by conforming to particular social class values based on social connections, economic resources, race, ethnicity, genders, sexual orientation, ablebodiedness, or education. Thus we are who we are due to the cultural dynamics of different social classes as well as historical forces.

Lastly, in order to understand the complexities of social changes more fully, social intelligence shows us that societies produce cultures that perpetuate themselves and accomplish vital tasks to meet societies' most basic survival needs. Societies also respond directly to populations' widely shared beliefs, social class divisions, and historical forces. Consequently, societies' cultures are vital syntheses of social influences that define options for individuals, communities, and societies.

This socially intelligent consideration of the complexities of social processes may initially discourage us from trying to understand cultures sufficiently to make cultural and social changes. However, we now understand more fully that cultures are the life-blood of societies, and that they make marked differences in how individuals, communities, and societies conduct themselves, especially in relation to social ideals like social justice. Therefore, social intelligence guides us to be more in charge of our destinies, through making different cultural choices as individuals, communities, and societies.

History and Cultures

Symbolic expressions of shared experiences and communications—such as artistic representations and cultural artifacts—existed for long periods of time before writing or refined mathematical skills were developed. For example, cultural symbols were used to express grief after family or community leaders died, during special community or religious funeral rituals. By contrast, comprehensive historical records are a relatively recent development in the cultural evolution of human beings.

Major cultural changes in communities were first recorded when members' lives became settled and stable, as well as when writing skills developed more fully. Often our earliest written records were related to heroic achievements, or to strategic aspects of political power, wealth, and success in conflicts and wars. Later, more mundane aspects of communities and community needs—such as counting populations or taking inventories of resources—were subjects of historical records.

According to contemporary conventions, examining written histories about peoples and events is a widely accepted means of authenticating social facts. Therefore, we often rely on histories to understand why some groups are engaged in particular activities today, for example, or why some civilizations did not thrive. From the viewpoints of social intelligence, history is an invaluable means to understand social realities, largely because of the emphasis given to facts in written histories. For example, we can now document major events in the past—such as political crises or natural catastrophes—through official written records, personal diaries, and symbolic interpretations of artifacts and art works.

History is also a reliable source of how people have thought about cultures and cultural changes, and it gives us ways to understand cultural contrasts or cultural conflicts. We not only get to know particular cultures better by examining their histories, but we also understand cultural clashes more realistically when we check historical records for culturally significant facts. We are who we are because of our shared histories, and because histories contrast with each other.

In these respects history gives us a sense of belonging to certain communities and societies, or makes us outsiders in relation to communities and societies. Our social well-being depends in part on how we think we fit into history, and how we assume our roles and responsibilities as historical actors. Social intelligence helps us to realize that we are all historical actors whether we know it or not, and want to be so or not. The questions we must answer for ourselves include whether we should accept our responsibilities as historical actors, with socially intelligent verve and imagination, or go in other directions to lead what we believe would be more enjoyable meaningful lives.

From these perspectives we realize that history affects our cultures deeply, and that history may determine some important aspects of our cultures. For example, when we are raised in war-torn countries, especially if battle conflicts are on our home territories, our world views and values are inevitably strongly or permanently influenced by these individual and shared experiences. Also, if we are children when wartime stresses occur, their impacts on our values and ways of being in the world are deeper than if we are mature adults.

In considering the effects of particular historical conditions on family cultures, we discover that the knowledge bases of our societies in part result from political and economic histories of societies and groups within societies. For example, histories of social class cultures show that social inequalities are deep-seated, powerful cultural and social influences.

When we consider social changes and cultures, and the extent to which cultures cause social or cultural changes, we must examine related historical facts. This enables us to question whether interpretations of these facts are socially intelligent or biased in favor of special interest groups such as political and economic elites. We can then decide whether the histories accepted by most people in our societies need to be debunked, revised, or rewritten in order to make more sense of cultural continuities in the present.

Social intelligence requires us to continue to question to what extent cultural and social expectations are based on conventional interpretations of historical facts. This enables us to resolve how we can best intervene in the powerful and complex processes of cultural changes, so that we are less deterministic in our thinking about the future, and about the destinies of particular individuals, groups, communities, and societies. For example, it is only by questioning others' interpretations of historical facts that we become sufficiently objective—as well as sufficiently free—to follow the guidance of social intelligence principles in understanding and dealing with powerful, complex cultural changes.

Materialism

Materialism is an important social value in contemporary societies. This social fact makes it useful to explore and understand some social origins and contemporary expressions of materialism. Although we can use history productively to accomplish this task, we also need to remember that social intelligence requires us to stay rooted in the present, rather than overly connected to the past. Therefore, we look at history primarily to inform us about the present cultural significance of materialism, for example, so that we can bring about changes in the cultures of materialism now, in order to influence societies that are overly dominated by materialistic values.

When we take broad historical views of cultures in social changes over the last three hundred years, we see that the industrial revolution had—and continues to have—strong impacts on our cultural values, and on social conditions in our societies. In fact, if we use one word to describe current cultural emphases in Western industrialized societies, especially in relation to globalization and other countries in the international community, we could choose "materialistic."

Materialism is a cultural belief system that supported the industrial revolution in its earliest stages, lasting to the present and foreseeable future. One result of materialistic belief systems is that we tend to cherish and value our possessions more than abstract values, such as truth, in our everyday lives. We see that material resources, like wealth, are passed down from generation to generation, and that gaining materialistic rewards now immediately benefits us, our children, and grandchildren. Furthermore, scientific and technological inventions in recent decades suggest that our well-being depends on purchasing goods and services.

Because we can become materially prosperous overnight, or in relatively short periods of time, materialism creates high expectations about possibilities that increase our material assets soon, so that we can enjoy the good life. Thus, materialism feeds enthusiasms—sometimes frenzies—to accumulate and spend our resources in ways which are not necessarily advantageous. For example, we are so intent on the production or consumption of material assets, that we easily lose sight of the broader pictures of our options and social realities.

Because materialism is a deep aspect of our contemporary cultures, we rarely consider that we have sufficient economic resources or material goods. The grip that materialism has over our awareness and sensibilities makes many of us constantly think and dream about material assets. Consequently, we tend to lose touch with our agency as historical actors, for example, because our worlds are largely experienced as striving to acquire tangible products or services. We feel compelled to achieve particular standards of living, even though we may realize some of the negative effects of our deep beliefs in materialism, or feel restricted and imprisoned by materialism.

Social intelligence offers us relief from the relentless pressures of materialism. Although it is clearly advantageous to be members of cultures and societies that value sufficient material goods to provide comfortable lifestyles and challenging opportunities—so that we and our families thrive and live fully—we may need to limit our consumption of material goods in order to control some of the impacts that materialistic cultures have on our individual and collective well-being. For example, when we focus more on critically assessing our experiences of materialism, our socially intelligent choices about how we really want to live become freer and more objective.

It is important to recognize the widespread dominance of materialism and material goods in our contemporary industrial cultures and societies. We avoid the predictable penalties of materialism best by aiming to be more socially intelligent, especially through cultivating and achieving goals that contribute to the common good. Therefore, rather than going with the flow of materialism, we build social and cultural conditions that increase individual and social freedom in the present and future.

We are more enlightened in how we live today when we put our materialistic yearnings to one side, for example, in order to decide what it is in the present that is most important to us. To the extent that our deepest preferences are new or re-emerging constructive values which others may share, our cultures can be catalysts in broad social changes.

Religions and Changes

Different religions influence our attitudes to self and others, as well as our identities, behavior, world views, and life outcomes. Because religions are made up of clusters of cultural symbols, meanings, values, and beliefs, religions are cultural forces in their own right, and can predispose individuals and populations toward mass societal changes, such as the industrial revolution and industrial development. In these respects religions are carriers of culture, and can be thought of as being in the forefront of new historical eras or as "causing" social changes.

On the other hand, religions can also be considered as essentially turning attention away from important social facts and social issues that consequently do not get satisfactorily resolved. By focusing on life after death, for example, or on the supernatural qualities of God, individuals and groups may be lulled into complacency by religious beliefs and rituals. This means that religious believers are often not sufficiently angry or motivated to improve their harsh cultural and social conditions. In these respects, religions become conservative influences that resist social changes. In fact, religions can be thought of as important sources of apathy or disinterest in bringing about changes that might challenge "God's will."

Although these views about the influences of religious beliefs in societies are not usually articulated by or for the masses within populations and societies, they reflect and represent some of the social tensions and social issues that develop around religions or particular religious beliefs and social change. Furthermore, these cultural and social dynamics tend to persist, because if we try to be more religious, we often deliberately remove ourselves from lively debates about new cultural or social changes.

Suffice it to say that religions are extremely powerful forces in societies, especially because they affect the lives and actions of whole populations. Because religions address the hearts and souls of individuals and communities, they speak to deep-seated concerns about our individual and social identities or fulfillment. When we decide to align ourselves with particular denominational religions, for example, we voluntarily accept social labels that suggest we are predisposed to their clusters of values, beliefs, attitudes, and actions.

Once we accept the fact that religions are powerful cultural forces, we see that some religious beliefs—or cultures—cause or promote distinctive social changes. However, because there are many differences in how the beliefs of individuals and groups are prioritized within the same religions, we see that our generalizations about cultures causing social changes are limited in predicting outcomes from belonging to certain religions. For example, we may only be able to conclude that some religious traditions seem to promote social changes more than others.

Social intelligence helps us to put these complexities in broad social perspectives, so that we both acknowledge the possible power of religions within cultures as promoters of social changes, and pay attention to the conservative impacts that religions have in inhibiting or slowing social changes. When we are socially intelligent we are alert, pragmatic, and realistic, so that we can be more astute in designing effective strategies to bring about cultural and social changes.

Another reason that social intelligence suggests that we should pay attention to the power of religions is that we introduce religions to our children at young impressionable ages. Furthermore, religions play emotionally significant roles in life-course rituals for births, marriages, and deaths, so we often follow in the footsteps of parents and grandparents in honoring particular religious traditions throughout our lives. Multigenerational religious influences are extremely difficult to change, because challenging well-established ways of doing things frequently disrupts our families.

Social intelligence suggests that optimally we need to critically review our religious beliefs, in order to have some control over the consequences of our religious beliefs for our lives. Because religious beliefs have powerful life outcomes, we try to ensure that accepting clusters of beliefs within particular religions really works for us as individuals and members of societies. However, social intelligence also suggests that if we find contradictions between our religious faiths and the social realities we deal with on a daily basis, we need to question or adjust our religious beliefs accordingly.

Social intelligence does not imply that we should abandon our religions, but rather that we need to interpret religions in meaningful ways, so that we can increase the common good and social justice more effectively. Whenever possible we benefit from preserving the support and wisdom of our religions, as well as from accepting the spirit of our families' religious and cultural traditions. For example, we are usually comforted, strengthened, and inspired by religions when we choose traditions within denominations that address our deepest beliefs about ourselves and the world.

Social intelligence principles enable us to make new adaptations to our religions. We may also choose to affiliate with other religions, or choose not to belong to any religions. Whatever we decide as socially intelligent individuals, we need to remember that religions are powerful cultural influences that are instrumental in bringing about major cultural and social changes. Even if we decide not to affiliate with religions, for instance, we inevitably continue to live in societies where religions are powerful cultural influences that impact the social conditions of whole populations and civilizations.

III. Cultures Cause Changes?

Secularization and Sciences

Secularization is often thought of as the opposite of religion, with the power of science being a major factor in bringing about a world that does not believe in God. Modernization and industrialization are also considered to be important aspects of secularization, which at the same time seem to have reduced the power and influences of social traditions and religions.

When we use evolutionary perspectives to understand the development of human societies, we find that traditions—such as preliterate customs—predate religions as we know them, even though wherever people congregated beliefs were important to survival and honoring remains of the dead. Thus, although religions predated most political regimes, traditions served as original sources for the development of our earliest religions.

To the extent that religions were founded from our most entrenched traditions, or from established ways of coping with the harsh exigencies of staying alive, religions were in turn gradually challenged by beliefs and ways of thinking that did not appeal to a supreme being, or to supernatural forces, as ways to explain the universe. Thus science and secularization have increasingly transformed both our traditions and religions in modern times, even though traditions and religions continue to be central aspects of our cultures.

Some religious leaders, philosophers, and social theorists predicted that religions will die at the same time that secularizing influences take hold in modern societies. However, religions have continued to exist alongside secularization, often in relatively peaceful conditions. Furthermore, sciences are now important knowledge bases for modern societies, which make some peaceful transitions in social changes possible.

Throughout history our increasingly complex societies have required us to use reliable knowledge to make successful adaptations to our geographical and social environments. Although sciences have challenged traditional religious, philosophical, and historical views of our worlds, we increasingly benefit from some of sciences' abilities to predict and manipulate our environments for our survival and fulfillment. For example, we can now realistically aspire to lead more privileged lives than our parents and grandparents, in part due to the rapid advances of sciences and technologies.

Because our societies are less mysterious than they used to be, we work hard, buy goods or services, and make our ways in a world that is more tolerant of diverse behavior. Furthermore, rather than being beholden to the religious dictates of our elders, we are freer to be whoever we want to be in modern secular worlds.

Thus secularization and sciences have transformed our cultures and values, often into products for consumption rather than ends in themselves. For example, although we may no longer want to pursue the truth, we can earn money to transform our ways of being and doing in the world. Although modern ways of being and doing are questionable and much debated, when we are socially intelligent we realize that complex modern trends predictably widen the ranges of our choices. Furthermore, such wide-ranging choices, when available to all, may gradually transform our cultures constructively, as well as improve the qualities of our lives for generations to come.

Our responsibilities as socially intelligent individuals are to see the power and complexities of our cultures and their social consequences. Our socially intelligent objectivity allows us to recognize—and use—cultures as ways to bring about more desirable social changes and globalization. For example, social intelligence helps us to see the many advantages of secular world views, which do not necessarily negate traditions and religions. Social intelligence is a secular way of seeing the world, which encourages us to be free as well as to seek social justice through making increasingly astute choices in our thinking, believing, and acting.

Although sciences do not always give us additional freedoms and choices directly, we can use social intelligence principles to regulate the dissemination of scientific information and techniques that benefit us the most. For example, social intelligence helps us to make difficult decisions and commitments about just ways to distribute the social advantages that sciences bring, which include increased access to education in the sciences.

Socially intelligent strategies make our societies less likely to get stuck in time warps which honor only well-established traditions and religions. Diversity in knowledge, as well as diversity in people, helps us to discover or design ways in which we can gain advantages from embracing secularization, sciences, religions, or traditions in our complex and powerful cultures and societies.

Cultural Innovations

Even though cultures do not bring about cultural and social changes through a simple cause effect transformation, cultures undoubtedly have significant influences among the complex social forces that bring about cultural and social changes. When we make cultural innovations in how we think, what we do, and what we accomplish with others, our cultural interventions are more likely to have effective impacts. More accurately, our cultural innovations are significant aspects of chains of events that lead to cultural and social changes.

We see from these sequences of events, that cultural innovations are invaluable, and that our choices of values and commitments make differences in the grand scheme of things. For example, when we emphasize value choices that are life-enhancing rather than destructive, we set cultural patterns and social influences in motion that move us toward increasing the common good and social justice. Although our cultural intentions alone are not sufficient to bring about changes, our lived cultural choices and behaviors affect our cultures and societies, whether we act alone or collectively.

Our most critical cultural innovations are in the social spheres of families, beliefs, social classes, cultures, or societies. These are the five major strands of social intelligence and sources of social facts, which have the strongest impacts on our lives. We are who we are because of the influences of these five major cultural and social forces, and we change who we are and what we accomplish through making cultural innovations in these five social spheres.

When we interact with our families, for example, we tend to meet others' expectations, and go with the flow of our families' cultures. Even though our families' cultures may be very different from our broader societal cultures, we usually want to "fit in" or "belong to" to our families' cultures. In order to bring new values and beliefs to our family cultures, however, we may be required to take stands which are less accommodating to our relatives, and less consistent with how things are done in our families. Furthermore, when our cultural interventions to modify our families' cultures are predictably resisted by our relatives, it is only when we persist in making cultural innovations—perhaps through socially intelligent persuasion—that our family cultures and families are changed.

Similarly, our beliefs may have to be deliberately modified in order to make innovations in our cultures. Social intelligence heightens our awareness of what we need to change—or want to change—in our beliefs, in order to make them more aligned with our deepest intentions and goals. For example, we may decide to make cultural innovations so that we are more effective in increasing the common good or social justice. Our socially intelligent awareness of our beliefs and values, guides us to create cultural innovations that reinforce our directions toward strengthening and increasing the common good or social justice.

We also design and create cultural innovations by changing our social class value choices. When we decide that we are no longer going to follow the social class values we were raised with, or to which we previously aspired, we free ourselves to make more flexible value choices and commitments. Our increased freedom from the restrictive influences of social classes frees or neutralizes other social class values we harbor, so that the overall power that social classes wield over us is reduced rather than reinforced. For example, we may decide not to be as passive as we were encouraged to be if we are women, or not as aggressive as we were encouraged to be if we are men. Thus, our gendered patterns of behavior and expectations benefit from being loosened up by cultural innovations, and we are able to work more effectively toward cultures that increase the common good and social justice.

Making direct cultural contributions are other cultural innovations that bring about cultural and social changes. For example, if we write novels about freedom or paint pictures about enlightenment, our artistic contributions impact the sum total of ideas, ideals, values, and expectations in our cultures. Artistic cultural contributions touch people's hearts and souls, and may increase whole cultures', societies', and civilizations' capacities to create social conditions for cooperative, peaceful coexistence among diverse populations.

History, or the progression of societies, is also affected by cultural contributions and cultural innovations. New ideas related to the care of children and the elderly, for example, create new trajectories for families and societies. Although cultural innovations such as munitions technologies often lead us toward the destruction of societies, the possibility persists that destructive cultural innovations can be neutralized and transcended by more constructive, life-enhancing cultural innovations. We have existential responsibilities to care for ourselves, others, and our planet, and we use social intelligence to help us to meet this need, especially by making life-enhancing cultural innovations in our societies.

IV. Past, Present, and Future Cultures

O ur past, present, and future cultures reflect the power and complexities of cultures in our families, communities, societies and civilizations. When we use broad socially intelligent perspectives to understand our everyday lives, we connect our local and global cultures to each other, in order to see the parts we play in defining and interpreting our past, present, and future cultures. This challenge stays with us as we increase our social intelligence and become historical actors, which enables us to gradually refine our values and value choices, so that we are more effective in increasing the common good and social justice.

Our past, present, and future cultures determine the qualities of our societies and civilizations. For example, we build essential ways of existing and acting on foundations of traditional or modern social facts, values, and expectations. We are social and cultural beings, whose cultures permeate all aspects of who we are and what we do, including our vital biological and physiological processes.

Social intelligence keeps us rooted in the present for the future. Although it is important to understand our present situations by examining the past, we cannot afford to stay focused on the past because our past social conditions have changed, and the present is the most real pathway we have to the future. It is imperative that we choose our most viable starting points in the present, watch where we are going, and stay on courses that lead toward our future goals.

Our trajectories from the past, in the present, and to the future are strongly influenced by our past, present, and future cultures. Even though political power and economic resources may seem remote from many of our cultural forms and processes, political and economic actions inevitably influence our cultures, and our cultures define possibilities for political and economic strategies. Furthermore our past, present, and future cultures are significant social influences because they express specific values, which affect the qualities or directions of social actions and social changes.

At the same time, our cultures influence the many ways in which we understand and value time as a priority or as something that is inconsequential. Because political strife or economic exigencies influence how we experience and value time, our priorities flow from cultural conditions in our particular situations. Social intelligence explains that many of our decisions to act or make commitments are value choices, and that our priorities consistently shape our value choices and their outcomes.

Social intelligence helps us to make sense out of the mass of value choices that confront us each day. Unless we use social intelligence to clarify our goals and priorities, for example, we may not be aware of the extent to which we need to deliberately consider values as we conduct our daily business with others. However, whether we are aware of our value choices or not, much of what we do and accomplish results from our cultural preferences about the qualities of our lives.

To a certain extent we may choose to deny the passage of time or the importance of time, because circumstances in past cultures influence our participation in present cultures. Nevertheless, in the long run, we cannot afford to ignore the effects of time on the meanings of our lives, our behavior, and our accomplishments. For example, being socially intelligent strengthens our capacities to use time for constructive purposes, so that we no longer allow others to distract us from our goals, or indulge ourselves in activities that divert our attention away from our highest priorities.

When we become more socially intelligent, we are more alert to the social consequences of our cultures and our cultural choices. This awareness connects us to our past, present, and future cultures, because changing cultures reflect and express shifting cultural emphases and values. Furthermore, when we are inspired by our past, present, and future cultures we increase the common good and social justice more easily and more meaningfully.

We understand complex nuances about our cultures when we are socially intelligent, so that we appreciate options and possibilities related to our past, present, and future cultures more fully. For example, social intelligence increases our freedom; we become more purposeful in making value choices; and we are forward-looking in our cultural preferences.

Alert to the Present

Social intelligence requires that above all we pay attention to our present social circumstances, and that we take responsible actions based on our awareness and understanding of our current cultural and social situations. Whatever broad perspectives we use in applying social intelligence to our everyday lives, we must necessarily live fully in present cultural conditions and the cultural contexts of who we are, where we are, what we have achieved, and what we want to accomplish.

Social intelligence requires us to assume responsibilities as historical actors as we go about our business with others in present cultural circumstances and situations. This means that even though we need to stay rooted in the present, in order to see our cultural choices and opportunities clearly, we must also address our present cultural options and challenges through historical perspectives. Therefore, we stay fully committed to resolving individual and social cultural issues of the present, and at the same time consistently take into account historical facts that enable us to understand the present more fully.

We stay rooted in the present in order to orient our behavior, decisions, commitments, and actions toward improving future cultures as well as present cultures. For example, social intelligence requires us to stay alert to the cultural directions we move in through our present actions, so that we connect our needs and yearnings to the consequences of our value choices.

Consequently, some of our present actions in current cultures are undertaken expressly to achieve long range cultural goals or cultural changes for the future.

Taking socially intelligent action in the present includes being aware of the past and future, as well as focusing on current cultures. We maintain broad perspectives in our current decisions so that we stay open to knowledge from the past, as well as to predictions of cultural trends or cultural goals for the future. We cannot risk being narrow-minded in following social intelligence principles, because this ultimately negates our intentions to increase our social intelligence. Only when we balance our actions through grounding them in the present, as well as connecting them to the past and future, do we increase our social intelligence through our behavior, assume responsibilities as historical actors, and work effectively toward achieving shared cultural goals to increase the common good and social justice.

The most powerful connections we have to our cultures, when we participate in these cultural and social change processes, are our choices in values and beliefs. When we deliberately orient our actions with selected values and beliefs, our actions express our cultural preferences. Our trial and error efforts to increase our social intelligence, and achieve our cultural goals, are continuously affected by how well we focus on our values and beliefs as we act. Ideally, social intelligence motivates us to change our values and beliefs if we are not making sufficient progress toward our cultural goals. For example, we need to continuously select constructive values and beliefs to guide our actions in our families, communities, societies, and globalization.

When we consistently stay in touch with the pulse of our present cultures, as well as with the momentum of cultural changes in our societies and the international community, we are more motivated to increase our social intelligence. Paying close attention to our present cultural orientations and value choices ensures that we do all we can to bring about more constructive cultures and societies. The depth and extent of our cultural awareness and cultural participation readies us to design cultural innovations, which improve qualities of others' lives as well as our own.

Experiencing broad cultural influences in our societies and globalization overwhelms us when we do not feel connected to the five major social influences of families, beliefs, social classes, cultures, and societies. When we continue to build our social intelligence—through paying attention to reciprocity and interdependence in families, beliefs, social classes, cultures, and societies—we sustain our connectedness to our cultures because we make more deliberate choices in our beliefs and values. For example, we remember that we are significant players in the construction of our cultural and social environments, and we realize that we are more effective in our accomplishments when we work cooperatively with others, even though we can achieve a great deal through our unique individual socially intelligent decisions, commitments, and goals.

Looking Through the Past

We look closely at the past in order to learn about the present, and to inform our socially intelligent strategies for improving the future. When we recognize that we are cultural and social beings, we learn a great deal about human nature and human possibilities by reviewing the past, especially our cultural and social histories.

Although most of us neither pause to think about our evolutionary origins when we go about our daily business, nor formulate specific goals for the future, it is necessary to cultivate a working knowledge of the cultural development of humans and societies in order to understand history, the present, and the future. Human beings have not become who they are in a vacuum. Social and cultural contexts of human development are critical influences on the emergence of both human limitations and human achievements as we know them today.

It may not be particularly inspiring to think of patterns in human behavior that predate our formal historical records.

However, hunting and gathering societies, as well as the earliest horticultural societies, show us how accomplishing particular cultural tasks were necessary for survival in these early stages of human development. For example, in preliterate times, cultural objects assumed symbolic meanings as well as social significance with respect to burials, wars, wealth, and personal possessions. However, because our early settled communities stayed relatively isolated from each other, they were slow to grow into larger settlements.

Acquiring a sense of what cultural priorities were in our earliest communities and societies makes us more aware that what we call "history" is relatively recent knowledge. For example, comparisons between our early historical societies and contemporary societies yield more similarities than comparisons between earlier evolutionary societies and contemporary societies. Once communities produced goods which went beyond their immediate survival needs, they settled and created cultural resources which in part served to regulate behavior within their communities and societies.

These views of the origins of communities help us to see that cultures have consistently been significant aspects of societies, especially once individuals' and families' survival needs are met. We also see that we use cultures to support us as our needs and wants multiply, for example, and that we need cultures to communicate effectively with each other.

Cultures are profound sources of inspiration, because they are evidence of our successful survival, as well as accomplishments that go beyond practical human needs when biological and physiological needs have been met. The development of rudimentary languages was a major turning point in the refinement of our cultures, for example, because clear and complex communications are the core of successful cultural adaptations from early historical times to the present.

Social intelligence requires that we strengthen our understanding of our historical origins by considering the growth of economic and political aspects of our communities, as well as the development of religions. Human beings need sufficiently accurate world views, for example, in order to make reliable assessments of their current circumstances, which are strongly influenced by economic systems, political systems, and religions. Although resources, power, and magical or religious beliefs were integral parts of our earliest families and communities, they often became increasingly dominant in history, and still define the world views of many populations in globalization.

Historical facts about particular eras are important strands of historical knowledge. However, for the purposes of increasing our social intelligence, it is sometimes more important to develop a general sense of our earliest histories. For example, we need to see how conflicts result from different world views and values in recent cultural and political histories, rather than stay immersed in detailed historical facts and narratives of the remote past.

Our capacities to examine the past, in order to see the present more clearly, largely depend on our interpretations of histories. We try to see the present through our histories, so that we understand the main cultural emphases that emerged during particular times. Being a socially intelligent historical actor means that we educate ourselves about past, present, and future cultures, so that we make more meaningful future-oriented value choices in dealing with present cultural circumstances.

Moving Toward the Future

Our cultures play critical roles in moving us toward the future, whether we are interested in establishing improved futures or not. Although ultimately it is our actions that count the most in influencing our future civilizations, our cultures feed our visions of how the world could be, our definitions of individual and social possibilities, our motivations, and our orientations to action. Thus our cultures define the most meaningful substance of what we bring into being in our futures.

Social intelligence helps us to understand the significance of our cultural choices in bringing about cultural and social changes. First, however, we need to balance our efforts to make particular cultural changes by realizing that, above all, we must remain deeply rooted in the present rather than the future. We should pay attention to pressing individual and family needs, for example, so that we do not act destructively in our current situations as we strive for new and improved possibilities for the future. This practical and humane grounding in the present saves us from being too urgent, or too insistent in our expectations for others as we try to create better futures.

When we consider broad views of cultural or social changes—one of the strengths of being socially intelligent—we assess what we should take from our past experiences to address the present and future more effectively. In these respects, our efforts to bring about improved futures do not derive solely from idealistic visions of possibilities, but from past and current ideals and social facts. Using past and present ideals and social facts, in our designs for new futures, makes our efforts to create improved social conditions more effective in the long run.

Looking closely at our past and present cultures enables us to see a broad array of traditions, values, meanings, ideals, expectations, knowledge, religions, legal systems, beliefs, languages, and dreams. Given these complexities, social intelligence helps us to appreciate the close associations between cultural and social realities in our everyday lives. When we see the power and pervasiveness of our cultures, for example, we are more selective in making value choices to motivate our actions. However, the omnipresence of our cultures makes it difficult to change our cultures, in part because we cannot grasp or control our cultures sufficiently.

Even though we may feel overwhelmed by the power, complexities, and presence of our cultures, to a certain extent we can continue to choose which cultures we create—or perpetuate—in the future. In spite of being restricted by our capacities to imagine cultural and social possibilities, social intelligence shows us how to stay practical so that we move our visions, plans, and designs into tomorrow's world.

IV. Past, Present, and Future Cultures

We create enlightened plans and strategies to accomplish goals for the future when we perpetuate the most life-enhancing aspects of our communities and civilizations. For example, we try to eliminate or reduce the harshest social conditions of social injustices in our societies by working toward constructive goals with others.

When we establish easier access to shared resources, more families thrive, and social class extremes in resources are minimized or replaced by alternative ways to organize our populations. Thus we actualize our hopes for the future by building new cultures based on social facts now. Consequently, when we work with people who value equality, inclusiveness, diversity, cooperation, and openness, our collective efforts create cultural and social conditions that constantly increase the common good and social justice.

Once we have viable designs or plans in mind, and are motivated to put them in motion, we act in ways that move us toward better futures. We depend on social intelligence to yield tools and strategies that make our collective efforts to build new worlds more effective and more enduring. For example, social intelligence helps us to use and change our cultures wisely by emphasizing values that we believe in the most, to actualize our visions of what our future cultures and societies could be.

The challenge of creating new futures makes us ever more aware of the importance of time in our societies, histories, and cultures. Because social intelligence is a pragmatic strategy, we need not only understand what time means in our cultures, but also stay aware of the importance of timing our actions and negotiations with others. Maintaining this level of awareness of time in our cultures helps us to make more effective choices in balancing our concerns about our past, present, and future cultures.

Time in Cultures

As our understanding of the centrality of cultures in our everyday lives grows, we see different ways in which time is valued by various societies, social classes, and groups, as well as in contrasting historical periods. For example, in contemporary modern industrial societies, we often associate time with money because wages for specialized workers depend on the time labored.

Time is also valued by cultures through assessments of the length of our lives. We may or may not value long lives, for example, but how we treat old people inevitably expresses the degree of respect or reverence we have for the lived passage of time. Similarly our contemporary emphasis on the value of "quality time" is almost a contradiction in terms—time itself is not valued as much as how we use time. For example, there is social pressure not to squander time, or fritter it away in casual relationships. Thus our modern fast-paced societies have increased our awareness of time.

Besides becoming aware of the centrality of time in our cultures, we need to consider broad cultural orientations to the past, present, and future within and among our populations. For example, members of upper social classes often value the past through their deep respect for traditions, usually because many historical traditions uphold privileges for upper class members. However, members of middle social classes benefit more from paying attention to opportunities in the present. They increase their social mobility by seizing current opportunities for education, occupations, and social advancements. By contrast, members of lower classes—such as immigrants in modern industrial societies—tend to orient their actions toward building better futures for themselves and their children. They try to establish cultural and social conditions that improve the circumstances and situations of their children in the present for the future as soon as possible.

The broad orientations that cultures and societies have about past, present, and future time are seen in the cultural and social influences of families, beliefs, social classes, cultures, and societies. For example, some families are closely connected to their families' histories and ancestors. They believe in maintaining continuities through different generations, and define the roles and responsibilities of current family members by stressing the importance of carrying family traditions forward for present and future generations of their families. Patterns in family inheritance express these cultural preferences, and family members often pay more attention to family cultures than societal cultures.

However, some broad cultural beliefs about the future may contradict families' beliefs in their own traditional family cultures. For example, societies' cultural beliefs are frequently reinforced by mainstream religions, politics, or education. Consequently, choosing to nurture beliefs that are markedly different from our families' cultures increases our independence from our families, especially when we associate with those who have contrasting beliefs.

Cultural beliefs that focus on using time may essentially take us away from our families' cultures, so that we establish a momentum for our lives that increases our emotional distance from our families. In these respects, it is not only the power of the content of our beliefs that establishes our orientations to ourselves and our societies, but also our attitudes toward time.

Social classes make us aware of how our families or friends change—or do not change—their statuses between the different generations of their families. We clarify our understanding of social mobility in our families, for example, when we see how social statuses varied in different generations of our families, and how particular family members had difficulties in establishing dependable paces of upward social mobility in our families and societies. As well as acknowledging that members of different social classes develop contrasting attitudes toward time, we see that we often measure ourselves and our accomplishments through time by making comparisons with others in our birth cohorts, or in similar generational positions as adults, parents, or grandparents.

Societies need to pay close attention to the passage of time when they are engaged in hostilities with other societies. Political threats to our security and survival are usually noted in historical records by specific times and places, as are our agreements to bring about peaceful conclusions to wars. Thus societies move through histories, at the same time describing and explaining major political events, so that our individual and family histories are forever changed by their connections to our societies' histories.

It is imperative to find ways to balance our cultural understanding of time, so that we establish effective cultural and societal priorities. We cannot ignore the past—we need to learn as much as we can from our past experiences—but we also cannot immerse ourselves totally in the future because of pressing current needs. Furthermore, how we value time in our cultures is frequently more significant than we realize. A well-established characteristic of social intelligence and our individual, family, or community maturity is that we make wise judgments about time and its effects on ourselves, our cultures, and our societies.

Denying Time

Social taboos about openly discussing the significance of death in our cultures show that societies often deny the importance of time. For example, we do not like to face up to the harsh reality that the length of our lives is limited, and that we eventually succumb to the relentless laws of nature by dying. Furthermore, our cultures show us that supernatural powers are usually reserved exclusively for God or gods, historical leaders of religions, or individuals blessed with extraordinary charisma. Beyond this we need to all find meaningful cultural explanations and practices, so that we cope effectively with our survival, fulfillment, time, and death.

We may deny time when we strive to be united with supernatural powers to lift ourselves out of banal ways of being that anchor us in historical time or evolution. However, because religious time often encompasses universal or eternal dimensions of our existence, religions may also move us toward broad spheres of individual and social concerns. For example, religions often make us confront questions about the purposes of our existence, especially in light of the timeless attributes of the God—or gods—we worship.

Whereas religious time focuses on the universality of human experiences and access to divine presence, historical time is largely the domain of secular concerns in contemporary societies. For example, historical records are a secular accounting of significant local and national events. These include births, marriages, and deaths, as well as the most memorable facts of our personal, family, community, or national experiences through time.

Evolutionary time, although sometimes considered as an integral aspect of some religions, is largely a secular or scientific way to explain the infinity of time, and its influences on the development of our geophysical and human worlds. Thus both historical and religious time may be more limited in scope than evolutionary time, which bases its knowledge on geological eons rather than the last few thousand years.

Because of the selectivity and relativity of religious, historical, and evolutionary time, we see that when we focus on any one of these approaches to understanding time, we deny other characteristics of time. Social intelligence shows us that we are often limited in understanding and communicating our knowledge of time, and inadvertently deny significant aspects of time. Furthermore, because most people in contemporary societies do not ponder time-related issues, we frequently take time for granted, without exploring our assumptions about time.

When we do not question our partial views of time, or are preoccupied with trying to slow down the passage of time, we deny the impacts of time on our lives. Although we cannot understand the significance of time in all circumstances, we need to reflect on the passage of time to avoid denying the most significant social realities of time.

To the extent that we pay attention to social facts that indicate the passage of time in our lives, we see that time helps us to make decisions and commitments to contribute to the common good. However, when we experience only the immediacy of our individual or family needs, we are less able to balance past, present, and future cultural influences in our decision-making and actions. Ideally we value time and preserve time as a high priority in our thinking about how we live, in order to embrace the realities of time each day.

When we live in time zones that do not touch the lives of most people—for example, by focusing on solitary religious rituals, past histories, or evolutionary eras of billions of years—we inevitably deny the importance of time in the present. Similarly, if we concentrate on staying young for ever by engaging only in youthful activities with young people, we deny the fact that time enriches our lives. Also, when we believe that our present modern societies are so advanced that we have all we need now, we deny the advantages that broader time perspectives bring.

Social intelligence requires us to assess our social situations through time, in relation to broad time perspectives. Our lives express time if nothing else, and time is one of the most basic foundations and facts of our human, cultural, and social existence. Although cultures have taboos about recognizing passages of time that are difficult for us to understand, such as the reality of death for all living creatures, cultures can also bring us out of unproductive denials of the importance of time. For example, works of art heighten our awareness of time, as do philosophies or moral treatises, so that we make more realistic cultural choices to acknowledge and honor time daily.

Using Time

Social intelligence suggests that we need to understand the role that time plays in our cultures, so that we use time for constructive pragmatic purposes, rather than perpetuate habits that deny the existence of time or waste this precious resource. Although we may be hard-pressed to find satisfactory ways to measure time, we can see that some degree of precision is necessary to make sufficient use of time, in order to increase the common good and social justice. Furthermore, it is because we are immersed in time, that it is difficult to be objective about time.

When we see the importance of time in bodily functions or music, we appreciate the fact that timing social interventions to build improved societies is a significant basic concern rather than superficial. For example, when we run our businesses effectively, timelines are necessary for evaluating sales strategies. We must use time wisely to develop business or social enterprises successfully.

Although we do not have to walk in lockstep with others, we should pay attention to how others see us and hear us through time. For example, we synchronize our efforts in projects, so that we move forward in rhythms that reflect our awareness and interests in cultural and social resources. We use time wisely when we see the purposes of our actions in historical, religious, or evolutionary contexts, as well as in cultural time perspectives. Consequently we are effective historical actors in complex and powerful cultures, who pay attention to broad time dimensions as well as to specific, local, or unique times.

When we are socially intelligent, we time our actions in order for them to have the greatest impact on us and others whenever possible. For example, we ask questions when we know that we can get answers, or when the questions serve particular purposes such as getting individuals and groups to think about how they conduct themselves and what they take for granted. We do not merely fill time, or pass the time of day, but rather have specific projects that we want to accomplish within time. Because we realize that we die all too soon, we choose to accomplish the most meaningful goals we have set for ourselves whenever possible.

These concerns address some of the urgency and immediacy of time in our lives. Although we may spend some time usefully contemplating the limitlessness and timelessness of the universe, eventually this is a diversion which does not allow us to make substantial contributions to the common good and social justice. Social intelligence teaches us to value the time we have, as well as to live fully and purposefully within our time limits.

Living fully, according to social intelligence, includes meeting our personal or family needs, as well as thinking and acting meaningfully in relation to the cultural and social conditions of our situations and opportunities. We try to live our answers to existential questions such as how to contribute the most to others, ourselves, and our families in order to spend our time usefully and fully.

Balancing our time perspectives, being creative historical actors, and increasing social justice are ideals that motivate us to continue in directions that increase social intelligence. We may also use other cultural ideals or metaphors to keep us moving in these directions, through making appropriate value choices. For example, we consider that we have missions in life, which help us to be aware of how to accomplish specific goals. Or, we may consider that we exist to do God's will in conducting our everyday lives. In addition, we may show others how cultures and social influences affect us deeply, often limiting rather than freeing us to live productively.

Our cultural choices in values and social ideals motivate us for lifetimes, and we influence others continuously. Ideally, our values and social ideals are sufficiently inspired to improve the worlds we live in, because they help us to see cultural and social connections among our families, communities, societies, and civilizations. Furthermore, we see that our restricted life-spans mean that we must work closely with others to achieve our most difficult goals. We do this not merely because cooperation is an effective way to do things, but because unless we work with others time will run out, and we will not have accomplished what we want to during our lifetimes and beyond.

V. Better Cultures

Because social intelligence is a method and a technique, rather than an end in itself, we must make moral, ethical, or value choices as we assess the content of our cultures, and the social conditions that our cultures produce. Whether we choose to apply social intelligence in the best ways possible or live without social intelligence, making value choices is an inescapable existential dilemma that we are compelled to resolve. Even though we may prefer to deny these cultural and social realities—which are integral aspects of our shared human condition—our value choices include deliberately selecting our values as well as evading or negating our cultural and social responsibilities.

Some cultures are best characterized as having values which tend to be either constructive or destructive. When we pay close attention to the power and complexities of our cultures, and aim to create better cultures, we see many ways to improve our cultures. For example, we may use principles of social intelligence to guide us in making productive value choices.

However, we also need to appreciate the fact that deciding to use social intelligence is a value choice, and that social intelligence can be used for either constructive or destructive purposes. In these respects, social intelligence is valuable knowledge that may be applied to a wide variety of individual and social ends. Although the most constructive purposes of social intelligence are emphasized in *Cultures and Social Intelligence*, dictators and other authoritarian leaders frequently use social intelligence to manipulate populations to meet their own egotistical needs and goals.

Just as cultures have either more constructive or more destructive clusters of values, they may also be either self-oriented or collectivity-oriented. Our values and cultures influence us to care only about success in individualistic terms—self-oriented cultures—or focus on the well-being of whole populations—collectivity-oriented cultures. Because capitalism has promoted many self-oriented cultures, social intelligence shows us that viable cultural alternatives emerge from deliberately designing and promoting collectivity-oriented cultures.

Cultures may also be life-enhancing or death-directed in orientation. When cultures concentrate on strengthening values that create healthy, rewarding opportunities for their populations, they are life-enhancing. However, when cultures emphasize values that are dead-ended, which lead to choices that do not meet the needs of their populations, they are eventually death-directed in orientation, moving toward the extinction of whole societies. For example, clusters of death-directed values may be expressed as lacks of opportunities, limited educational facilities, inadequate health care, or the neglect of critical life-stage needs during infancy and old age.

Given such contrasts in cultural possibilities and cultural choices, with related patterns in values and individual or social consequences, we see that cultures are important social influences that predispose populations to act in certain ways. Because we are consumers and creators of cultures, we have the freedom and responsibility to choose—as wisely as we can—which values to incorporate in our everyday lives, especially when we realize that if we go with the flow we are more likely to create undesirable cultural and social conditions in the status quo.

Social intelligence helps us to identify clusters of values in our cultures, as well as the momentums of our cultures, so that we discern and predict some of the social consequences of our value choices. Social intelligence principles fortify us to stand up to the tides of destructive, self-centered, or death-directed cultures that harm our well-being, so that we build more constructive, collectivity-oriented, or life-enhancing cultures to increase our social intelligence, the common good, and social justice.

Social intelligence shows us that if we want to change the meanings and momentums of our cultures to promote the well-being of whole populations, we need to build cultures that express constructive, collectivity-oriented, or life-enhancing values. When we include these innovative values in our everyday decision-making and actions, we counter the strong influences of destructive, self-oriented, or death-directed values. Ideally, we find like-minded others who work with us toward positive goals, so that we bring better cultures into being.

Some of the value choices which bring about better cultures are equality, inclusiveness, diversity, cooperation, and openness. These cultural values gradually improve the quality of social conditions in societies and the globalization of our local cultures. Because these new values are so vital for improving societies, we take a closer look at their impacts in the rest of this chapter of *Cultures and Social Intelligence*.

Equality

Historically, equality has been a political slogan for many social, cultural, and political reforms. Even though equality is often confused with sameness, lack of differentiation, and robbing people of their power or privileges, equality can also be viewed as a constructive, collectivity-oriented, life-enhancing value choice. Because all cultures reinforce specific value choices, power relations, political options, and political consequences, cultures that emphasize equality necessarily express specific aspects of value choices, power relations, political options, and political consequences.

Cultures that stress equality are founded on beliefs that all individual members have similar basic rights, privileges, and power. When we move from hierarchical cultures with clearly defined elites to more egalitarian cultures, we often describe and explain this transition as reorganizing power and resources. However, equality does not deprive individuals or groups of what they need. For example, when social justice is an important priority, cultures of equality promote a shared understanding that people have many similar needs and desires. In this spirit, the cultural value of equality helps us to address problems of adequate resources for whatever it is that human beings need to be fulfilled.

Equality does not mean that standards of living necessarily decline, but that high standards can and should be maintained for all rather than a few. The promise here is that when we deal with our populations more equally and more fairly, productivity and fulfillment predictably increase. Also, new products and services are explored in egalitarian cultures, because more people have opportunities and receive just rewards for their labors.

The specific cultural changes involved in achieving equality in cultures and societies are not easy to accomplish and vary widely. However, when we face in directions that increase equality within and among populations, we are more likely to build better cultures and better futures than if we nurture clusters of values that are destructive, self-oriented, or death-directed.

Cultures that espouse equality as a central value predictably loosen the hierarchical ordering of their social classes, so that there are increased opportunities for members of lower social classes. For example, families and beliefs that previously supported social class structures—often without individuals' awareness that they were doing so—become effective agents of change when they promote equality within and among cultures. Furthermore, when family dependencies are less hierarchical, family members are freer to pursue constructive goals to increase the common good and social justice.

As well as being a political value, equality is a personal value. Adult intimate relationships, family bonds, and friendships are healthier and more mature when they are based on equal rather than hierarchical values. Even though it appears that some hierarchical relationships exist among other mammals and animals, humans have created cultures and civilizations with wider ranges of life-enhancing choices and possibilities. For example, many of us choose to express the value of equality in our personal relationships, in order to improve the quality of give and take that is necessary for mutual understanding, empathy, and personal fulfillment.

Social intelligence endorses the cultural value of equality, in that equality creates more flexible social conditions for the achievement of widespread opportunities and better futures. For example, societies that incorporate the value of equality in their cultures create fewer alienating conditions, and produce less prejudice and discrimination. Although transitions to equality inevitably precipitate some new social problems, these are possible to solve because overall we are moving in constructive, collectivity-oriented, life-oriented directions.

A socially intelligent strategy to promote the value of equality in our cultures is to realize that other social influences are needed to reinforce equality in cultures. We pay attention to equality in our families, for example, so that genders and sexual orientations are no longer restricted by unequal power relations, prejudices, and discrimination. Thus whenever possible we rise above our self-interests to address collective needs. Similarly, we cultivate different ways to be equal, so that our beliefs are more focused on equality as motivations for our individual and collective actions.

Social intelligence encourages us to design new ways to organize our societies, so that the cultural value of equality takes root in our social structures, without being negated or neutralized by social classes. When we deliberately build our communities and our societies on cultures of equality, we become stronger collectivities in adapting to social changes, and designing or creating better cultures and futures.

Inclusiveness

Inclusiveness is a second cultural value that predictably brings about better cultures. Inclusiveness is a collective valuing of all kinds of people, whatever their race, ethnicity, social class, education, religion, gender, sexual orientation, age, health, or ablebodiedness. Valuing inclusiveness means that we do not exclude individuals or groups from benefiting from the common good, so that the rewards of our shared accomplishments are distributed among all individuals and groups. When we express the cultural value of inclusiveness we also accept and embrace cultural, social, and physiological differences among people, rather than merely tolerate or put up with these differences.

The cultural assumptions made in valuing inclusiveness are that when we reduce prejudice and discrimination in our cultures, our societies are more humane, less alienated, and less conflicted. Furthermore, when sufficient public opinion prioritizes and values the tolerance and acceptance of all individuals and groups, we are less likely to perpetuate prejudice and discrimination. For example, all individuals and groups tend to pursue the common good when inclusiveness is valued. Also, increased satisfaction about social situations and living conditions allows people to imagine more constructive goals as they work together to create better futures.

One of the significant social facts of social intelligence is that societies need the contributions of all members of their populations, so that they can create preferred social structures and social processes. Although social intelligence suggests that whole societies have more power and influences over our lives than the sum total of individuals within societies, valuing inclusiveness emphasizes that we need each individual in society to contribute as much as possible to the common good, so that we create and enjoy the best of all possible societies.

Social intelligence encourages us to understand inclusiveness from the points of view of our personal lives, communities, societies, and globalization. However, when we study the social facts of our situations and their social contexts, we are quick to conclude that we are far from experiencing the social value of inclusiveness at present.

This social fact should not discourage us, however, because first we must first see the truth of our situations, in order to make realistic commitments to change our current cultures. Furthermore, social intelligence assures us that realistically it is sufficient that we face in directions of increasing inclusiveness whenever we can. This eventually moves us toward making specific life-enhancing cultural changes, which gradually accept all individuals and groups in our societies.

In some respects, our new cultural value of inclusiveness flows from our previous acceptance of the new value of equality. In fact, there is considerable reciprocity between the two cultural values of equality and inclusiveness. For example, we cannot have true equality among people until we nurture inclusiveness throughout our populations. Similarly, we cannot have a viable inclusiveness in our cultures and societies unless we accept principles of equality among all people.

Other cultural values that predictably create better cultures—diversity, cooperation, and openness—cannot emerge as widespread cultural influences without establishing cultural foundations of equality and inclusiveness. For example, we do not appreciate diversity in its many manifestations unless we have sufficient viable conditions of equality and inclusiveness. Valuing cultural diversity is often hollow and meaningless, unless we have already laid sufficiently solid cultural foundations of equality and inclusiveness.

Cooperation and openness—the remaining cultural values that predictably bring about significant improvements in the well-being and functioning of our societies—represent a valuing of particular social processes in our everyday lives, social policies, and institutional arrangements. However, we cannot create effective long term cooperation and openness in our cultural and social exchanges until we are committed to emphasizing and establishing the basic cultural values of equality, inclusiveness, and diversity.

Singling out specific social values does not predictably create better futures, however, because this depends on societies' cultural preferences and traditional cultures. Nevertheless, social intelligence teaches us that it is important to focus on the particular values we want to change—individually and collectively—to create better cultures.

Although equality, inclusiveness, diversity, cooperation, and openness are often difficult-to-define abstract values, we benefit from keeping these cultural ideals in mind. For example, when we deliberately use constructive cultural values to motivate or orient our individual and social actions, we are markedly more effective in the cultural and social results of our actions, than when we act without this degree of cultural awareness and intention.

Diversity

The cultural value of diversity expresses deeply shared appreciations of the many gifts and talents that different people bring to our cultures and societies. The scope of cultural diversity includes considerations of our own societies, other societies, and contrasting civilizations. For example, social intelligence emphasizes the importance of recognizing the extent to which our social innovations and artistic creativity depend on valuing cultural and social diversity, because our strengths depend on the many ways in which we accept and benefit from rich varieties of human beings.

We see cultural diversity in the five major social influences of families, beliefs, social classes, cultures, and societies. Even though we may think that our own families are homogeneous, when we look closely at patterns of behavior in past generations, we often find relatives who married outside their races or religions, who transgressed social class traditions to travel abroad, or who became experts in foreign languages and cultures. When we consider the contributions that these individuals made to our family cultures, we see that other relatives benefited from these new contributions to their family cultures.

Similarly, when we look at the beliefs that we and others use in our everyday lives, we find that some beliefs are influenced by relatively "alien" experiences. For example, as young adults we frequently "try out" a rich diversity of beliefs in order to get to know what our own beliefs are. In addition, systematic exposures to others' beliefs are often achieved through education, and in large part becoming well-educated means that we gradually eradicate our individual and collective ignorance and bigotry, so that we truly enjoy and benefit from cultural diversity.

Because social classes are built on hierarchies of cultural differences and contrasting cultural meanings, we recognize that we already have much diversity within and among our social classes, whether these classes are based on social connections, financial assets, education, religion, race, ethnicity, gender, sexual orientation, health, ablebodiedness, or age. For example, we have cultures that vary depending on the ages of individuals and groups, as well as on the historical cohorts into which we are born. Similarly, genders and sexual orientations have cultures which contrast with each other, as well as with the cultures of social classes based on economic assets.

Social intelligence shows us that although establishing social class hierarchies is often how we have historically recognized and dealt with diversity within our populations as well as among our cultures, societies, and civilizations, we do not need to perpetuate traditional social classes to control or restrict diversity. Valuing cultural diversity may be a step toward redesigning or reorganizing social classes, for example, so that the cultural diversity we already have is inclusive rather than exclusive, and based on principles of equality.

We see what diversity is most clearly when we consider the wide variety of cultural expressions of uniqueness in our cultures. Furthermore, the cultural facts of diversity are more self-evident than the pragmatic usefulness of valuing cultural diversity. Thus, although we may agree that modern societies are characterized by cultural diversity because we see diversity in our everyday lives, we often need to be persuaded that cultural diversity is a constructive social value that brings about better cultures and societies.

Diversity can be thought of as a foundation of modern societies, whether we acknowledge this social fact or not. For example, our most powerful global cities are based on extensive cultural diversity, and it is largely cultural diversity that stimulates the imaginations of artists, entrepreneurs, and politicians to produce richness in the city life of modern societies.

Because there is no escape from cultural diversity in modern societies, diversity is here to stay. Our existential challenge is to cultivate our most positive individual and social attitudes to welcome and embrace cultural diversity, so that we can use this richness to enhance our everyday lives.

When the cultural foundations of our societies are made up of values of equality, inclusiveness, and diversity we are more prepared to cooperate with each other, and to be open, forthright, and honest in our individual and group communications. These are values and qualities of life which create more constructive cultures and social conditions, so that we live fully, increase the common good, and achieve social justice. Our cultures must be sufficiently powerful and complex to create outcomes and successes along these lines, or they will hold us back from achieving such vital improvements.

Cooperation

Although it is easy for us to think of examples of competition, it is more difficult to recall as many instances of cooperation. This suggests that competition is more of a core value in our contemporary cultures than cooperation. For example, we may agree that cooperation is both possible and effective, but we also realize that most of the time our cultures emphasize values related to competition rather than cooperation.

When we watch young children—or animals—playing, we see that competitiveness is readily evoked. In order to understand our shared competitiveness, we acknowledge that we have established many formal and informal ways to compare and contrast our behavior. For example, we compete for attention or in order to get even minimal rewards, sometimes without realizing that we are competing with others. Furthermore, the extensive cultural substructures of capitalism and the global market economy are based on the power and values of competition among both producers and consumers.

When we focus on cooperation as a constructive, creative cultural value that brings about better cultures and improved societies, we often assume that cooperation will substantially replace competition as a way of getting things done in our societies, even though historical social facts suggest that this may not be possible. For example, in order to achieve cooperation in our day-to-day transactions with others, we need to concentrate on initiating cooperative patterns of interactions and transactions before customary competitive behaviors override our intentions. Furthermore, because *Cultures and Social Intelligence* proposes that equality, inclusiveness, diversity, cooperation, and openness are cultural values that predictably create better cultures, cooperation may be thought of as developing from the social conditions of equality, inclusiveness, diversity, and openness.

Human survival depends on others as well as ourselves, so cooperation usefully expresses our necessary interdependence, as well as the successful teamwork we develop with others in order to complete important or necessary tasks for our families and communities to survive. Furthermore, when it is obvious that our goals transcend our individual capacities, we are obliged to understand others' ways of acting and working. We embrace both cultural similarities and differences when we cooperate with others to accomplish shared goals.

For example, we often cooperate in our families to meet our families' needs. Cooperating in assuming these responsibilities provides family members with basic survival and fulfillment necessities. Although we may at the same time experience intense competition in our families, such as sibling rivalries, we know that most of the time we count on cooperative spirits in our families, in order to move along effectively with the business of life. Our capacities to build mature personal relationships in our families are based on being reliable and dependable in our exchanges with others, so that our cooperation is ultimately expressed as efficiency and productivity.

We are more likely to cooperate with others when we accomplish tasks through sharing and maintaining similar beliefs, such as religious beliefs. Similarly, the give and take required in discussing our shared religious beliefs is another form of cooperation. Moreover, we may create communities of learning around cooperative exchanges in our shared tasks and beliefs. Such cooperative reciprocity prevents our beliefs from dying or from becoming less meaningful. Therefore, when we build organizations and communities around cooperative political or religious beliefs, better cultures are established which may endure for long periods of time.

Above all, we try to build cooperation into our cultures by understanding the importance of cooperation in achieving our goals, by establishing conditions for cooperation in our schools and other social organizations, and by valuing cooperation in our new and old social traditions. We try to extend and perpetuate cooperation in our cultures by pursuing goals with likeminded others, for example, and by educating publics about the significance of working together to achieve particular goals. Thus, we make known the social intelligence principle that we achieve our goals most efficiently and most effectively by working with others cooperatively, rather than by working alone or being competitive.

When we examine cooperation historically in our societies, we find that we developed institutional ways to accomplish our goals by building legal systems. Our laws often try to enforce cooperation, because there is usually less interest in cooperation than is necessary to get most people to cooperate. However, if we deliberately use cooperative ways of learning and behaving in our schools, for example, adults are more inclined to cooperate with each other to achieve shared goals, especially when the tasks in hand are difficult and demanding.

All in all, we need to remind ourselves of the socially intelligent fact that cooperation is learned, and that as such cooperation can be learned and relearned from generation to generation. The possibility that we can produce future generations of individuals and groups who prefer to cooperate rather than compete with each other remains. However, we also need to create inspiring or meaningful social conditions for cooperating with others, so that ultimately a culture of cooperation enables us to accomplish our cooperative work better.

Openness

When the first two new values for better cultures—equality and inclusiveness—impact the structures of our families, communities, societies, and globalization, the new process values for better cultures—diversity, cooperation, and openness—are more likely to develop. For example, social intelligence draws our attention to the importance of cultural and social patterns of interaction in the power and complexities of cultural and social influences. Furthermore, social intelligence helps us to understand that social structures, such as social classes, emerge from many repetitions of the same cultural and social processes, and that one way to change social structures is to initiate variations in patterns of social and cultural exchanges.

When we focus on the cultural value of openness, we change our ways of relating to cultural and social influences. For example, seeing closures in our social systems of families, beliefs, social classes, cultures, and societies makes us aware that these conditions are not ideal in our societies, and that we benefit from creating individual and group processes that open up our patterns of communications, as well as our formal and informal group memberships.

Openness is a cultural value which in part derives from patterns of communications and actions. When we value openness, we increase directness and cooperation in our exchanges. Openness also increases our clarity in social and cultural practices, making it more possible to share cultural ideals, goals, and strategies with others. Thus, the cultural value of openness makes us pay attention to the qualities of our exchanges with others, so that we work together more effectively by taking stands against secrecy, negative coalitions, and other subversive strategies which block progress toward constructive goals like increasing the common good and social justice.

Openness helps us to get on the same side in our endeavors, so that we bring progressive cultural and social changes into being. Consequently, we create better cultures that increase our individual and shared social intelligence. Some of the differences that valuing openness makes in our cultures are understood more fully by examining contrasts in openness in the five major social influences of social intelligence: families, beliefs, social classes, cultures, and societies.

For example, families that do not value openness tend to be dysfunctional, especially in the long run. Family communications that harbor secrets and alliances block the capacities of these families' emotional systems to be supportive. Furthermore, closures in families' exchanges prevent them from establishing reliable patterns of interactions that meet their ongoing daily needs. Closures in families' exchanges, especially after major emotional events like deaths in families, divide the flexible relationships needed to create viable family emotional systems. Ideally families use open exchanges and open communications to develop adaptive bonds.

Similarly, viable beliefs need openness. Maintaining openness in our beliefs honors a spirit of inquiry, as well as strengthens access to knowledge from outside sources. When we close our beliefs and belief systems, our beliefs become incestuous in that they cannot of their own accord produce new ideas, or create new ways of doing things. We must necessarily stay open in our beliefs so that we continue to learn and change our behavior throughout our lives, as well as increase our social intelligence.

When we cultivate the value of openness in relation to existing social classes, we increase social class mobility, as well as create options for organizing populations in alternative ways to traditional social classes. Valuing openness changes the cultural underpinnings and social processes that maintain social classes, and gradually replaces social classes with better alternatives.

Cultures are critical for sustaining openness because they are sources of new ideas, and provide fresh inputs for assessing our actions and strategies. Also, when we accept openness as a cultural value, we protect our democratic rights to participate actively in public issues. Actualizing our democratic rights is a direct benefit of cultural openness, and valuing cultural openness encourages us to use a wide variety of cultural sources to inspire our motives and actions.

Societies are responsive to their populations when the cultural value of openness is well-established in social institutions like governments and legal systems. For example, when sufficient people are concerned about keeping social systems open, they protect their freedoms and increase their capacities to make decisions in their everyday situations. Consequently, openness increases possibilities for fair treatment and social justice, in part because vested interests are more readily dissipated in open societies.

We conclude from these sketches of outcomes from applying the cultural value of openness to contemporary societies that openness supports healthy cultures and societies. Openness is also a principle of social intelligence, which helps us to gain information and objectivity about our everyday situations and strategies. When we review possibilities for incorporating new or different values in our cultures to bring about constructive cultural and social changes, openness is a powerful cultural and social influence in its own right.

Value Choices

Ultimately, our easiest and most direct means to bring about effective cultural and social changes is to make different value choices. However, individual value choices alone are not as effective or as powerful in their impacts as collective value choices. Just as individuals can conduct their lives according to the principles of social intelligence, groups, communities, and societies can use the principles of social intelligence to guide their actions and strategies, especially to make significant changes like establishing new cultural values or priorities.

When we look only at our families, we see that our relatives act differently according to the emotions they invest in particular values. For example, family members who are invested in establishing the value of harmony in their family relationships may find sharp limits in these desired ends, because we cannot consistently control the emotional well-being of other family members. By contrast, family members who have goals and commitments outside their families are often more able to meet goals both outside and within their families, due to their value choices of freedom and autonomy in many different social situations.

What we do with our lives—as individuals and as groups—results largely from the values we cultivate, and the values we engage in through our commitments. Social intelligence helps us to see the significance of value issues in our families, beliefs, social classes, cultures, and societies so that we are more aware of our value choices, and more thoughtful about the consequences of our actions. For example, we are more effective historical actors when we understand the value choices that we make in relation to our cultures and societies.

Value choices can transform a life that is dull and listless into one that is zestful and meaningful. We have to decide for ourselves which values we want to pursue in our lives, for example, particularly if we want to make contributions that create better cultures in the present and future. Therefore, it helps us both individually and socially if we can clarify—for ourselves and others—what our value choices are.

When we interact with members of the youngest generations of our families, we become more real when we single out and describe which values we stand for, as well as why we stand for them. For example, children are often interested in how we go about making our decisions, and how we see our families and social worlds. Our goal is not to make our children and grandchildren like us, but rather to help them to understand that values make a considerable difference to our lives. Furthermore, valuing freedom in our exchanges with our children needs to be an integral part of these exchanges and communications.

Whereas some of our value choices in relation to our families, beliefs, and social classes may seem to be personal rather than social, the more we find objective or universal aspects of values related to our families, beliefs, and social classes the freer we are in interacting with others. When we are socially intelligent we consider families, beliefs, and social classes in broad social perspectives. This opens up our belief systems, so we are more objective and more discriminating in our personal and social value choices.

Thus, there are always public or broad social dimensions of our personal lives. In fact, considering that our lives are unique and personal may entrap us, because we fragment our understanding of the social influences that impact our lives. However, when we make commitments to increase our social intelligence, we necessarily open up and scrutinize broad views of our current situations, their pasts, and our futures.

Considering the social influences of our cultures and societies broadens our perspectives on our lives, even though we sometimes find it difficult to understand that what we do in our cultures and societies affects us and others. Social intelligence helps us to realize that the broadest social influences—such as globalization—impact our lives in significant ways, and that it is up to us to assess in what respects we want to adapt to or challenge these influences through our value choices.

Our value choices serve us well in many respects. We become more socially intelligent when we make deliberate value choices, and we are also more successful in accomplishing our goals when we make deliberate value choices. For example, we are more likely to lead others when we are effective historical actors, because we express our value choices directly through our actions. Furthermore, considering the particular value choices of equality, inclusiveness, diversity, cooperation, and openness helps us to clarify our ongoing value choices and achievements in relation to better cultures and social justice.

Social Intelligence and Cultures

VI. Social Intelligence Perspectives

Social intelligence is defined in many ways, and is used in countless situations. Although we are born with social intelligence, and develop social intelligence as children in order to survive, we may also choose to strengthen and increase our social intelligence as adults, which benefits us directly as well as others. *Cultures and Social Intelligence* emphasizes the choices we can make to increase our social intelligence and benefit others as well as ourselves.

Social intelligence is a tool that helps us to see ourselves and our societies more clearly and more objectively. Social intelligence is also a working knowledge of social facts with principles which guide us when needed, so that we are aware of social influences, objective in our assessments of complex social situations, decisive in our commitments, and effective as historical actors.

Social intelligence helps us to be pragmatic in our approaches to everyday life, so that we find viable ways to accomplish our goals, seek out like-minded others to help us to achieve our goals, and pursue meaningful long range goals like increasing social justice. Social intelligence provides us with broad perspectives on our social situations—especially through the prisms of the five major social influences of families, beliefs, social classes, cultures, and societies. Using these broad perspectives increases our objectivity, and frees up our choices, decisions, and commitments.

Social intelligence guides us in assessing the impacts of families, beliefs, social classes, cultures, and societies on our lives, and helps us to be more discerning in how we make value choices in relation to our families, beliefs, social classes, cultures, and societies. For example, we learn how to question the assumptions we make about our genders or sexual orientations, so that we gain objectivity and broaden our ranges of options for decision-making and commitments. We also use social intelligence to see ourselves as historical actors, who consider resources—including time—responsibly in order to increase the common good and social justice.

Social intelligence helps us to be who we want to be in ways that we prefer. For example, we become more deliberate and more astute in designing strategies to accomplish our goals, and whenever possible we work with others because this makes our contributions more far-reaching and effective.

Social intelligence encourages us to make changes in our cultures and societies, so that the world becomes a better place for more members of our populations. Freeing tasks—such as reducing the negative impacts of social classes for lower social class members—may become missions as we continue to increase our social intelligence. Furthermore, even the slightest changes we accomplish make significant constructive differences for us and others.

Social intelligence helps us use our current assets and given situations, so that we make the most of our advantages without impinging on others' rights. For example, we increase our social intelligence so that we not only meet our family needs responsibly, but also aspire to make substantial contributions to the common good.

Our imaginations are freer to design alternative social influences and social structures when we increase our social intelligence. We are less downhearted when our successes in achieving these goals are not apparent, so that we persist in our efforts to reach them. Furthermore, social intelligence teaches us that we need only face in directions of our social ideals, such as social justice, and act accordingly, rather than feel compelled to accomplish our goals now come what may.

Social intelligence gives us real hope—not false hope—for our futures and the futures of our cultures and societies. For example, when we focus on increasing our social intelligence, we are motivated to accomplish our goals in the long run. The tasks involved in increasing our social intelligence neutralize unrealistic concerns about achieving our goals to change our cultures and societies. Thus, when we keep our minds on the power and complexities of the social influences of families, beliefs, social classes, cultures, and societies, we are more effective in increasing our social intelligence and social justice.

Social intelligence helps us to nurture new futures where we value equality, inclusiveness, diversity, cooperation, and openness, so that all members of populations benefit from societal resources rather than only members of upper social classes. For example, we gain or maintain our freedom as sexual beings, by clarifying and claiming rights for our genders and sexual orientations. Furthermore, social intelligence helps us to maintain this cultural awareness, so that we create better futures from the present in which we live.

Families

Whether we are interested in cultures or not, our families are foundations of our social intelligence. We see our cultures primarily through the eyes and biases of our relatives, who select values from societies' cultures for our families' cultures. Sometimes religions play crucial roles in educating children about clusters of values and beliefs, which may be reinforced in adulthood by families' continuing religious practices and religious observances.

Members of past generations of our families played significant parts in selecting and repeating our families' values through our family cultures. We are born into ready-made family cultures—which continue to grow and change—so that our initial encounters with our family cultures necessarily include indirect cultural contacts with our ancestors.

Families are important because they lay foundations of our social intelligence. For example, our families' impacts are strongest when we are young and impressionable during our development as children and adults. From infancy, we interact in particular patterns of family dependency and family exchanges, which ultimately result in views and ideas about ourselves, our families, our communities, and the world. Our orientations to life—especially our significant emotional postures such as being active or passive in attitudes and actions—derive from the impacts that our families' emotional systems had and continue to have on our values, attitudes, and behavior.

Similarly, our understanding of morality, such as our initial definitions of right and wrong, results from the impacts of our family cultures, as well as patterns in our family dependencies and interactions. Even though very young children often have a clear sense of fairness—perhaps due to family dynamics in sibling rivalry or relationships with parents—it is through the languages and symbols of families' and societies' cultures that we learn to discuss morality and moral values. For example, families deliberately engage their children in religions, education, or leisure pursuits—such as reading classical children's literature—where countless issues of right and wrong in everyday life are emphasized and personified.

The fact that our families' cultures predispose us to spend lifetimes expressing loyalties to particular sets of moral values is important. It demonstrates the power and social or emotional significance of our families, as well as the social and emotional effects of morality for qualities of life. Consequently, social intelligence shows us that we are social beings, consumers of cultural values, and morally responsible agents in our decisions, actions, contributions, and life outcomes.

The breadth of social intelligence perspectives suggests that we are inevitably entwined with the cultural priorities of our families, and that these values are reinforced by our communities' or societies' views of the social and emotional significance of our families. For example, because societies expect families to socialize their children, which includes their cultural socialization, the emotional restrictiveness of family or parental leadership in these spheres often dominates children's lives, leaving them relatively little flexibility for exploring their situations. In the best of all socially intelligent worlds, however, children are encouraged to be independent in going forward in their lives, so that they make their own cultural and moral choices as much as possible and as soon as possible.

In teaching their children about right and wrong, some families distinguish between constructive or destructive cultures, self-oriented or collectivity-oriented cultures, and life-enhancing or death-directed cultures. Depending on the intensity of emotional dependence in their families, some children react by rebelling rather than accepting their parents' guidance about cultures. Nevertheless, because social intelligence teaches us that we must live our values rather than merely discuss them, children in socially intelligent families are encouraged to express their values directly in their everyday actions.

Social intelligence emphasizes that our families are our most important and most powerful sources of cultures. However, the content of the values, ideals, and cultures that families communicate to their children is often less influential than the emotional dynamics of their family dependencies. Therefore, we use social intelligence principles to become more objective about our families and their cultures, so that we are more responsible in making independent value choices in our families' cultures. This accomplishment gives our children more freedom to develop mature ways to understand and express cultural values and morality.

In some respects, our mature cultural preferences separate us from the intensity of our families' togetherness, which underlies our families' cultures. When children are well-educated, for example, they are more likely to pursue academic interests successfully as young adults, which increase their cultural opportunities. Families often support their children in these quests, because relatives tend to respect—although they may not understand—their children's intellectual interests. Social intelligence principles eventually help these children—and their relatives—to broaden their families' cultures.

Beliefs

Many of our cultural beliefs result from our ongoing family dependencies, as well as from our social class values, cultural values, or societal values. Social intelligence considers beliefs to be a major social influence in our lives—along with families, social classes, cultures, and societies—partly because of the power and emotional content of individual and social beliefs. Social intelligence shows us that we often go so far as to define social realities and our particular social situations through our beliefs, rather than according to social facts.

Social intelligence makes us more objective about our families, so that we discern more clearly the extent to which we allow our families to dominate our definitions of ourselves and our worlds. We frequently live up to our families' expectations for us, for example, rather than carve out independent purposes or directions for our lives. Furthermore, our paths of least resistance automatically duplicate relatives' patterns of interdependence, unless we deliberately seize our independence through making freer decisions and commitments.

We increase our social intelligence by examining the social and cultural origins of our beliefs. This loosens the grip of beliefs that no longer make sense in our lives, or that contradict those beliefs we care about the most. Social intelligence requires that we essentially edit our beliefs—by discarding beliefs we no longer want to honor, for example—so that our beliefs become more coherent meaningful cores of our attitudes and actions. We also substitute new constructive beliefs for those we discard, knowing that we need beliefs to motivate and orient our actions, as well as to connect us to broad currents of cultural and social values.

Our beliefs derive from clusters of values, as in religions or sciences, as well as from our family dependencies. For example, family influences are instrumental in defining which particular clusters of values we are exposed to, and encouraged to accept. Furthermore, family influences on our selections of values and beliefs are especially powerful when our relatives incorporate these clusters of values and beliefs in their own lives.

VI. Social Intelligence Perspectives

Social intelligence educates us. When we increase our social intelligence, we reduce our ignorance about the social consequences of holding particular beliefs through education and social intelligence, as well as heighten our responsibilities for our beliefs. Although not everyone who is well-educated applies knowledge to their beliefs, knowledge can help us to clarify or change our beliefs. For example, knowledge makes us more able to use the beliefs we choose to motivate and orient us to accomplish our missions of contributing to the common good.

Our beliefs are gateways to our family cultures, societal cultures, and other cultures. Social intelligence makes us ever ready to change our beliefs, because our beliefs are critical to understanding social realities and social facts. Social intelligence is built on a working knowledge of social facts, which helps us to ensure that our beliefs work for us rather than against us. We are more discriminating in choosing the beliefs we eventually call our own, for example, because we understand the broad social and cultural dimensions of our beliefs, as well as our existential needs to believe.

Our beliefs are cultural syntheses, which are starting points for designing more productive or more meaningful futures. One way to accomplish better futures—for ourselves and others—is to change our beliefs, so that they reflect future possibilities as well as past and present realities. We stay focused on creating better cultures and cultural emphases, for example, so that we deliberately choose constructive beliefs and values for our futures. We cannot design viable alternatives to the past and present unless we modify our beliefs, so that we both face up to and deal with the future more effectively.

Eventually, we must decide which beliefs we want to pass on to others—to our children and grandchildren, as well as to people we do not know. Are we sufficiently committed to particular beliefs so that we would stand by them in most circumstances? Are we ready to modify our beliefs to accomplish our preferred goals? Are we willing to assume responsibilities for the social and cultural consequences of our beliefs?

Social intelligence shows us that these are important questions to ask, whatever our cultural or social situations. By heightening our awareness of the social and cultural significance of our beliefs, we decrease negative impacts of ignorance, and increase commitments to achieve social justice. Because the value choices we make about our beliefs are experienced for generations to come, we should not take our responsibilities to hold one belief or another lightly, especially if we are to live fully and have peace of mind.

Social Classes

Our social classes are upheld and reinforced by specific social class cultures. These beliefs, values, ideals, ideas, knowledge, and expectations perpetuate the existence and functions of social class structures. Even though we may engage in economic reforms, such as redistributing economic assets in more egalitarian ways, the fact that social class cultures have existed over long periods of time means that social classes are very difficult to modify or eliminate.

In many respects our social class cultures need to be modified first, if we want to change our social classes. For example, when we have new attitudes and new perspectives on social classes, we are in better positions to make strategic changes in social class structures, including more egalitarian redistributions of economic assets. Therefore, our social class cultures are often the cutting edge of cultural changes that have significant economic and social consequences for whole populations.

Social classes are important influences on our cultures, because there are many social class differences in how people think, how they are educated, and how they live, as well as in how they receive and spend their financial resources. Social classes are complex organizations of populations, and they influence—usually by restricting rather than freeing—deep aspects of our being and doing.

We neutralize some dubious or harmful aspects of social classes and social class cultures through changing our general beliefs and values, as well as our specific social class beliefs and values. For example, when we reorient our priorities, we essentially ignore or neutralize some of the general and social class beliefs that used to define cultural expectations for our life outcomes. Thus the broad perspectives and increased objectivity of social intelligence make social class cultural changes possible and desirable, especially when we continue to develop our social intelligence.

One of the most significant consequences of increasing our objectivity, through becoming more socially intelligent, is that we increase our options in value choices, and do not succumb as easily to perpetuating family traditions of loyalty to particular social classes. When we realize the extent to which our social classes are human and social products, they lose some of their mystifying power and complexities. Consequently, the fact that social classes have existed in some form in all societies throughout history, does not necessarily mean that we have to conform to their restrictiveness and traditional expectations now or in the future.

Even when we realize that social classes may be based on education, religion, race, ethnicity, gender, sexual orientation, health, or ablebodiedness in modern societies, we are not necessarily beholden to these current trends, and may design alternative ways to organize our populations. Social intelligence emphasizes the importance of having freer social classes, as well as recognizes the option that social classes could be neutralized or redesigned.

The choices involved in designing new social classes, or in designing societies without social classes, are value choices. Social intelligence shows us that we benefit more from developing cultures which embody alternatives to existing social classes, for example, than from continuing to build cultures that support social classes as they are, that reinforce existing social inequalities and injustices.

Traditional social class structures are changed by globalization. For example, relatively recent international social classes are based on status differences between developed and less developed countries. However, these social class differences tend to be economic rather than cultural. Moreover, some material and economic differences among countries appear to make the functioning of the global economy smoother, because new divisions of labor—through outsourcing or migrations—have redefined and refined global market forces.

Overall, global cultural influences have perpetuated the dominance of Western cultures, rather than the independence of less powerful cultures. The material cultures we associate with capitalism typically overshadow traditional cultures, for example, because middle class consumer cultures are increasingly dominant in modern societies and globalization.

Social intelligence helps us to identify these important trends and nuances in social classes, social class cultures, and globalization. For example, we see the powerful, complex impacts of capitalism and capitalist cultures in global as well as local perspectives. Moreover, to the extent that we prefer global influences to be less materialistic, we must change our national and international cultural priorities, so that we address some of the cultural consequences of capitalism for social classes more directly.

Cultures

Cultures are made up of wide ranges of symbolic communications, which include visual images as well as verbal accounts. Our values, ideals, ideas, expectations, meanings, languages, education, legal systems, religions, knowledge, and beliefs are also integral parts of our cultures, for example, which help us to make sense of our lives and our societies. Our views of our cultures are biased by our earliest experiences of our families' cultures, but as adults we are inevitably confronted with new aspects of wider societal cultures many times each day.

VI. Social Intelligence Perspectives

We cannot escape cultures because they are omnipresent. Cultures are expressed in our dreams, and in our interpretations of our dreams, for example, as well as in banal aspects of our everyday lives. Cultures also underpin our histories, social classes, education, and attitudes toward education.

Education—such as increasing literacy throughout populations—is a reliable means to effect large scale changes in our cultures and societies. Education opens up new worlds, particularly by reducing our ignorance about social situations. Also, accumulations of knowledge give us power, as well as practical means to improve social statuses—for individuals and societies—in complex globalization processes.

Cultures play dominant, initiating roles in modernization, especially through mass communications and education. When we pay attention to the content and meanings of our cultures, we gain some degree of control over the cultures we produce. Social intelligence is a tool for individuals, groups, communities, and societies to use in intervening in what would otherwise be relatively automatic, unenlightened social influences. By emphasizing the importance of cultures—family, community, societal, and global cultures—social intelligence makes constructive contributions to understanding and modifying some powerful and complex aspects of cultural and social changes.

Although social intelligence emphasizes the importance of all five of the social influences of families, beliefs, social classes, cultures, and societies in the status quo and social changes, culture is often considered to be the most viable means to construct individual and social changes. For example, social intelligence sees cultures as distinctive and important determinants of change, or as blocks of resistance to change. Although families, beliefs, social classes and societies are also instrumental in accomplishing complex and powerful social changes, acting deliberately through our cultures often yields more innovative ways to impact the qualities of our lives and societies.

One of the most critical ways to influence cultural and social outcomes through our cultures is the value choices we make. For example, as individuals and as societies it is necessary to establish priorities for our survival and fulfillment in distributing varied resources. Making decisions about our priorities is particularly significant for our cultures, because our priorities are value choices. Therefore, recognizing and deciding what our priorities are inevitably expresses our most important values.

When we draw others' attention to our choices in our cultures, particularly in relation to establishing our priorities, we increase our shared social intelligence. We are more likely to act wisely, with astute considerations of our social situations, when we consider seriously what our priorities are or should be. Consequently, ethical and moral issues are raised in decision-making, which leads our cultures and societies in new directions when needed.

The emphasis social intelligence gives to value choices in our decisions makes cultures more significant in socially intelligent considerations and deliberations than in conventional thinking. Social intelligence pays attention to the extent to which human beings are dominated by their emotions—for example, vested interests are often based on emotional investments in particular traditions or social classes. Emotional investments in particular priorities show us our limitations in making objective, rational decisions. However, to the extent that social intelligence encourages us to be more reasonable about out emotional inclinations, we ultimately gain more control over our cultural inputs and outcomes.

Using the socially intelligent broad perspectives of families, beliefs, social classes, and societies makes us more objective about our cultures and cultural preferences. Being objective increases our abilities to see options in these broad social spheres, as well as balances our views of the past, present, and future. Continuing to increase our social intelligence motivates us to persist in our trial and error approaches to applying social intelligence in a wide variety of everyday social situations, so that we benefit directly from the pragmatic consequences of being socially intelligent.

Above all, social intelligence helps us to make reliable and effective interventions in our cultures, especially when individuals' and groups' needs are not being met. When we become more deliberate historical actors, and act in ways which increase social ideals such as social justice, we make more critical cultural assessments and decisions for better futures. We are more likely to accomplish our most cherished cultural goals, at the same time that we contribute to the common good or social justice, and increase our life satisfaction.

Societies

Societies are the broadest social influences on which social intelligence focuses—together with families, beliefs, social classes, and cultures—in order to understand the impacts of the most significant social systems on individuals and populations. Societies are particularly broad in scope because they include concerns about nation states, national and international histories, blocs of nations, and globalization. During the past two decades, for example, societies have become more global—partly through global cities—due to the global economy that simultaneously affects the international community and blocs of nations.

These broadest social contexts for defining human dependencies help us to understand the interplay of the social influences of families, beliefs, social classes, cultures, and societies. We see different strands of these significant social influences more clearly in relation to each other, when we examine how whole societies interact or deal with the influences. Furthermore, the perspectives of past, present, and future come alive through broad historical views of societies.

Looking at societies allows us to assess shared patterns in social changes, such as industrial developments, political systems, trends in civilizations, the world spread of religions, varieties in democracies, and migration patterns, as well as distributions of power and resources. Even though we still consider our own national needs as priorities, a significant social reality is that we are parts of global systems, whether we like or accept this social fact or not.

Social intelligence upsets traditional ways of viewing the world, not just when we use social intelligence to rethink difficult situations, but also when we are pragmatic about utilizing our more or less fixed shared resources to meet challenges in ongoing needs and circumstances. For example, even though we may have been born in privileged countries, our ever-pressing current social reality is that we live in a world where there are many countries which are not similarly advantaged.

Therefore, not only do we have ethical decisions to make about distributing our resources, but we also have to consider how we can best survive and be fulfilled in the long run, given the pressing needs of our own populations and other societies. Societal perspectives of social intelligence are means to assess our priorities, so that we understand that the common good relates to the international community as well as to local communities.

For example, social intelligence stresses the significance of the widespread emotional and physical needs that families have. Consequently, socially intelligent policies give primacy to the real needs of families—in our own countries and in the international community. Similarly, because education usually transforms the thinking of those who are taught, policies which improve the quality and outreach of education are instrumental in changing local or national conditions, as well as international situations.

By requiring us to examine societies' characteristics and needs, social intelligence broadens and educates our senses of responsibility. For example, we no longer think only of our own interests as central in assessing the well-being of our societies. We understand more fully that world conflicts arise due to international injustices, or perceived injustices, and that ultimately we need to act to resolve international conflicts and global problems as well as local situations. Social intelligence helps us to realize that when we examine only our own needs, we necessarily develop biased, self-centered views of the universe, which cannot effectively address some of the most critical everyday realities of globalization.

Because social intelligence is based on empirical facts, it yields practical knowledge and know-how that can be used in a wide variety of social situations. For example, social intelligence has principles that apply to societies, as well as to families, beliefs, social classes, and cultures. Furthermore, even though we seem to participate in particular ongoing social and historical changes because we have to, rather than because we want to, being more informed—or more enlightened—helps us to stay alive and make strategic decisions to increase the common good. Assuming such broad socially intelligent perspectives increases our life-satisfaction as well as helps us to survive.

Social intelligence shows us that we are all historical actors, whether we know this or not, and whether we work toward increasing the common good or not. We are active or passive members of the world community merely by virtue of being alive. Moreover, choosing to apply social intelligence principles increases our enlightenment as historical actors, so that we work expressly toward increasing the common good and social justice. For example, when we are sufficiently socially intelligent, we incorporate the broad perspectives of societies into our daily routines, so that our decisions about our everyday situations are objective rather than parochial.

Socially intelligent historical actors pay attention to present circumstances and the future, as well as to the past. We are historical actors to the extent that we align ourselves with the broadest influences of changing societies and globalization, which are history-making in their impacts. We also take advantage of the knowledge we have built from social intelligence to motivate and guide our actions, so that we are responsible in our interventions with others.

Social Justice Goals

Social intelligence views social justice as series of moral purposes which increase our socially intelligence. Rather than aspiring merely to cultivate social intelligence for its own sake, social justice is considered to be one of the most worthwhile ways to apply social intelligence in our everyday lives. We become socially intelligent in order to increase the common good, for example. By so doing, more people benefit from rewards and resources that were previously reserved only for members of upper social classes.

Social justice is also a practical ideal. Not only does social justice translate into significant everyday strategies, but it also suggests that the world benefits when everyone's needs are considered, rather than the needs of only a few members of privileged upper social classes. Thus, social intelligence shows us that our happiness and fulfillment depend on the extent to which we meet the needs of others as well as our own.

Social justice ideas permeate our families. Fairness is a perpetual cry from young children, for example, as they challenge the ways in which they are treated compared to their siblings. This is not to say that these children's claims are justified, but rather that we need to be sensitive to the rights of family members, as well as establish ethical standards in our personal relationships. Social intelligence requires us to be authentic in our dealings with other family members, which means that we must consider how we interact in these intense, personal spheres of interaction.

Social justice also guides us to decide which beliefs are most important to us. If we are committed to nurturing constructive beliefs, for example, we are more likely to act in favor of increasing social justice. Similarly, when we increase our social intelligence, we harbor beliefs which are collectivity-oriented and life-enhancing—qualities which predispose us to act in socially just ways.

Social justice is a moral compass which directs our efforts to decrease the most extreme inequalities expressed in our social classes. When we aim to achieve social justice, for example, we design more appropriate alternatives to social classes with regard to opportunities, social class structures, and ways to organize populations that go beyond traditional social classes.

Social justice clarifies our purposes and directions in constructing cultures that create better futures. However, we must also believe that our futures can be improved by particular measures. For example, when there are more opportunities for all, increased numbers of people will take advantage of cultural resources like education. Improved qualities of life also reduce alienation and political unrest in our societies, as well as increase social justice.

Social justice applies to whole societies. For example, we establish priorities about accomplishing certain social changes after we consider whether or not particular societies have sufficient social justice. Although we can increase social justice in many different ways, one starting point is to decrease extremes of poverty and wealth in some societies. Thus social justice is a moral compass that guides our socially intelligent efforts to increase and redistribute the common good.

Lastly, we find social justice when we examine the broadest pictures of our lives in trying to be objective. When we understand the broad social contexts of our interactions with others—in our families and societies—we move toward improving our relationships with ourselves, our families, and people we do not know. These broad views help us to assess the qualities of our social bonds, as well as increase social justice.

Socially intelligent broad perspectives let us see our options more clearly, which allows us to design meaningful constructive changes for social justice. Being objective reduces the emotional intensity of our vested interests, so that we address social justice concerns more directly, rather than remain fixed in narrow social biases.

These values and applications of social intelligence show us how social justice serves us well as an ultimate goal in increasing our social intelligence. In order to ensure that our social intelligence is used for the best purposes possible, we use social justice as a moral ideal to guide us in applying socially intelligent principles. By contrast, social intelligence is limited in its results and aims, because it is primarily a means to an end. However, social intelligence is also an under-rated, effective means, which can be depended on to accomplish social justice.

VII. Families and Beliefs

Families and beliefs are important foundations of social intelligence, as well as crucial influences in the formation and functioning of cultures. Because families and beliefs orient us to ourselves, others, and the world, they are critical dimensions of our early development and later behavior as adults. Many of our value choices, for example, flow from the emotional and intellectual influences of our families and beliefs, with the result that we inevitably participate in our families' and societies' cultures in biased or prejudiced ways.

Our families' patterns of dependence influence how we think about our social worlds, as well as how we absorb beliefs that we come to call our own. When we are children, we are virtually plunged into our families' emotional systems, which are both intense and difficult to manage. In spite of the fact that even as very young infants we may find ways to protect ourselves from some of the negative impacts of our families' emotional dependencies, our families' influences endure and continue to affect us in some respects throughout our lives.

It is amidst this enmeshment of family dependencies that we begin to believe something about ourselves, others, and the world. We may not be aware of how we formulate our beliefs, or how they affect our behavior, but they gradually become orientations and motivations for our actions. Furthermore, whatever beliefs we absorb from our families, especially when we are young, depend largely on patterns of dominance or emotional intensity in our families.

It is in this complex and powerful reciprocity between our families and family members' beliefs, that we develop awareness about our values and priorities. For example, we usually establish our bearings in relation to our families' emotional systems of dependence and independence, through first conforming to the emotional and moral mandates of our relatives, particularly those of our parents. These are significant beginnings of our moral development, which often become lifetime foundations for our adult behavior.

Patterns of behavior we experience in our families—especially repeated dependencies—express tensions between family togetherness and our unique individualities. When we are children we are urged or coerced to conform, but when we are adolescents or adults, we frequently rebel against these emotional and social pressures. Thus, our families' dynamics are catalysts in our absorption of our families' values and principles of right and wrong. For example, we develop our beliefs through our families' communications of our families' cultures, which are necessarily filtered through our families' dependencies.

Social intelligence helps us to understand the complexities of these family origins of our moral development, so that we cope more effectively with tensions between us and our families' pressures in our past and present value choices, as well as in our strivings to be independent through our value choices. By emphasizing the importance of achieving freedom, objectivity, and independence, social intelligence guides us to question and change those beliefs we accepted from our families which do not serve us well.

Social intelligence not only shows us the importance of understanding the earliest origins of our families' conditioning and families' influences on forming our beliefs, but also draws our attention to the fact that we need to change some of these foundations of our being if our value choices do not work well for us. Social intelligence heightens our awareness of the reactions our families predictably have in relation to our changes, and of how we can neutralize their restrictive impacts in the difficult processes of changing our cultural orientations to ourselves, others, and societies.

Our families' cultures, as well as more general societal cultures, are lasting sources of cultural values. We usefully renew our orientations to ourselves, others, and the world by getting immersed in alternative cultures and values, so that we make more socially intelligent choices in our values as we go about our daily activities. Social intelligence shows us that we achieve and maintain objectivity by making value choices in broad social contexts, which enable us to express cultures that contribute to the common good and increase our fulfillment.

Even though our families and beliefs persist in being strong influences on how we view our cultures, once we increase our freedom in relation to our families' dependencies, we make more effective value choices. For example, we use social intelligence principles to guide us to achieve independence through our cultures, so that we make deeper commitments to increase the common good and social justice.

Moral Development

Social intelligence shows us the impacts of patterns of dependencies in our families. We are who we are in large part because we are influenced by long term emotional styles of interacting in our closest family relationships. We have been and may continue to be embroiled by these dependencies, so that it is often extremely difficult to free ourselves from their impacts.

It is in such problematic conditions that we internalize our families' beliefs as our own. Our families' beliefs are communicated to us in a variety of subtle ways—through conversations, actions, and interactions about family events, family routines, and family crises. Consequently, we usually absorb our families' dominant beliefs, the particular beliefs of dominant family members, or the beliefs of our closest relatives, for example. Most importantly we accept beliefs about right and wrong in these family exchanges and interactions.

Even though we do not usually develop moral awareness about us, others, and our worlds in a focused way, our participation in our families' emotional processes is set in motion in our early years and continues for a lifetime. For example, we readily pick up nuances from what our relatives say and do in relation to others. Thus emotion-laden information becomes a foundation for our moral understanding and cultural preferences.

We may begin to discern principles of fairness through our parents' interactions with us and our siblings, although our impressions and ideas about fairness are also rooted in other emotional dependencies in our families. For example, even if we experienced our parents' disciplining practices as unfair, we may have fought against our brothers or sisters rather than our parents. Thus our early assessments of what is fair or unfair in life are frequently based more on emotional dependencies in our families than on intellectual moral principles.

Regardless of how we develop more independent moral standards when we are adults, social intelligence recognizes that our families continue to strongly influence how we distinguish right from wrong, and how we make value choices. Therefore, in understanding the importance of our families as cultural and social influences, social intelligence prompts us to acknowledge the emotional bases of our earliest and continuing value choices and moral behavior. For example, we are frequently so emotionally invested in our moral values, due to the early and continuing impacts of emotional dependencies in our families, that unless we free ourselves from these emotional biases we repeat them in varied social settings.

Our emotional and moral orientations to life are significant forces in our cultures. We are not objective, detached, or impartial when we are exposed to moral values as children. Because we need to survive and thrive in our families' emotional systems, we have to make sense out of our everyday experiences. For example, as children we depend on adult family members to sustain us, and many of these patterns of dependency may be prolonged into adulthood, even though we develop other family or personal relationships. Due to the fact that human beings are interdependent, social intelligence is essential for our long term, mature individual or social survival and fulfillment.

VII. Families and Beliefs

Another characteristic of the power and complexities of our families' cultures, and of how our families influence our beliefs and moral development, is the multigenerational continuities in our families' cultures. Sometimes the moral bases of our family cultures are communicated through family histories which go back for several generations. This means that family stories play significant direct and indirect roles in our moral development. For example, when we are children moral values are often presented to us through the life experiences of predecessors and ancestors. Therefore, because our families view some deceased family members as more successful than others, our families' opinions are strong influences over our moral judgments.

If a great deal of attention is given to families' ancestors and traditions in our family cultures, our value choices often seem clear but restrictive. For example, the privileging of particular aspects of our families' histories enhances the power and influence of biases in our families' cultures.

Consequently, although we may understand our value choices better through our families' cultures, we often feel suffocated by relatives' agreements about our ancestors' moral achievements and their expectations for us. We do not want to hear about what our relatives think we should do with our lives, for example, but rather long for freedom. Sometimes we express these strong yearnings more directly on later occasions, by rebelling against our families' cultures or by becoming more socially intelligent.

Because sharing our families' histories intensifies family togetherness, it may be difficult for us to make alternative value choices to the values of these families' cultures. In any event, we tend to continue to identify with our families' biological bonds. However, social intelligence shows us that although blood links and kinship are emphasized in many families' cultures, families are distinctive small groups because these memberships last for lifetimes and beyond, often due more to their emotional dependencies than to their biological origins. For example, if we are adopted into families, we become equal participants in these new families' emotional systems and cultures, so that we share our families' cultural and moral development influences equally with other family members.

Value Choices and Independence

When we are objective about our social situations, we neutralize some of the emotional intensity of our families' cultures, so that we see more cultural choices than before. Social intelligence helps us to choose values that are in our long range interests, for example, rather than values that merely endorse our families' cultures or ethnocentricity. Thus, social intelligence enables us to make commitments to values that increase the common good and social justice, rather than values that reinforce the status quo.

In coming to understand social intelligence and the power of social influences in our lives, we value freedom and autonomy more than before. For example, we come to terms with the complexities of the social influences of families, beliefs, social classes, cultures, and societies by placing a high priority on securing and maintaining freedom in our everyday decisions and experiences. Furthermore, we accomplish this by staying as objective as possible in our thoughts and actions about our value choices.

Our families and beliefs are two areas in which we tend to sacrifice our freedom in favor of preserving our families' togetherness. We often try not to rock the boat in our families' emotional systems, for example, by living up to our relatives' expectations. We also try to maintain or sustain our beliefs and our family beliefs, so that we continue to fit in with how things are done in our families. However, taking compromising positions to maintain the status quo usually does not increase our social intelligence, but rather strengthens our complacency about our existing family dependencies and family beliefs.

By contrast, if we commit ourselves to increasing our social intelligence, we place our highest priority on being independent and preserving our independence. For example, we carve out new routines to meet our needs for the freedom to think clearly and act autonomously. Consequently, making new value choices promotes our continued freedom and encourages us to accomplish goals that increase social intelligence, the common good, and social justice.

This process of claiming freedom for ourselves is expedited by examining specific patterns of control and freedom in our families. When our family members tend to restrict the freedom of children and other relatives, it may be difficult to seize our freedom. However, in the best of all worlds, although perhaps not a reality in some families, there is sufficient freedom to create flexible family bonds with other family members, so that a broad give and take in family and kin exchanges is enhanced rather than tightened. Social intelligence shows us that these flexible family emotional systems are healthier and more durable than rigid, brittle family bonds.

Social intelligence also teaches us that making value choices which support and express our independence must remain a high priority throughout our lives. Although we may readily choose freedom initially in order to increase our social intelligence, maintaining this momentum and habit of being needs to be a lifetime goal, even though we want to accomplish other objectives.

Our value choices and freedom are directly linked to both our family dependencies and our beliefs. When we create freer pathways for ourselves throughout our families' emotional systems, we become freer agents in a wide variety of social settings. Social intelligence derives from the social fact that achieving freedom in our families is usually a precondition of gaining freedom in other social ventures. Being free and independent in our families is vital, because it strengthens our capacities to be clearheaded and creative in all social settings. For example, unless we are free and independent, we cannot use our capacities to make social innovations through applying social intelligence principles.

Similarly, we need to establish freedom in our beliefs in order to let our beliefs motivate our behavior effectively and responsibly. For instance, we are braver and more courageous in applying our social intelligence, when we see what needs to be done in our social situations. When assessing what we should do, however, we cannot passively accept the status quo, or acquiesce to the negative impacts of existing family or social influences. We must act freely if we are to free others, as well as be less restricted by the power and complexities of the social influences of families, beliefs, social classes, cultures, and societies.

Thus, we create freedom in order to be independent. Because freedom is a scarce and valuable condition which may not be achieved easily, we cannot afford to ignore it, take it for granted, or neglect it by going about our daily business as usual. Freedom, independence, and responsibility depend on each other, and it is not possible to have one without the others in the long run.

Although it sometimes seems difficult to be responsible when we realize how many value choices we have with respect to being free and independent, we are moved in this direction by existential challenges to live more fully. This impetus fortifies our efforts to increase our social intelligence, enlarge our freedom, and continue to earn our independence through responsible free actions.

Questioning Beliefs

When we begin to free ourselves in our families, we question our beliefs more effectively. For example, we take a step back from our busy lives in order to reflect more deeply about what is really going on in the give and take of our family interactions, so that we can identify the most meaningful patterns in our family exchanges. Furthermore, we need to carve out sufficient family freedom for ourselves, largely through actively taking charge of our lives, before we can identify the dominant beliefs that hold our family cultures in place.

Because our beliefs are entwined with other family members' beliefs and ways of doing things, the act of questioning our beliefs may eventually challenge or interrupt customary behavior in our families. Business is no longer conducted as usual, for example, if we refuse to act automatically, especially when some established patterns of family behavior have existed for many years, sometimes for generations. Even if we begin to question issues that seem to be relatively minor, our questions may reveal new patterns of dominance in family exchanges, as well as new ways to relate to family members.

A healthy questioning of our beliefs often starts without any special purpose like increasing our social intelligence. The most fertile time to raise questions about beliefs in our families—that is, when questioning seems to be more appropriate or more natural—is during family crises, such as the deaths of significant family members. Re-examining families' histories in the aftermath of a family loss, or questioning who should take charge of matters related to this death, are practical issues that must be resolved. Family members are usually more open to thinking differently about their concerns during upheavals in their families' emotional systems.

Because families are both needy and vulnerable during family crises, family members' responses to factual questions may be more open and more forthcoming than if there were no crises. Furthermore, other family members are frequently more inclined to ask and answer questions during family crises, because there is considerable disorientation to established ways of doing things at these times. This is true whether family crises are precipitated by deaths, illnesses, births, marriages, job changes, unemployment, migrations, adult children who leave home, or assuming responsibilities for family members' special needs.

Questioning our families when there is no family crisis, especially about relatives' beliefs as well as our own beliefs, may appear to be confrontational. For example, asking for information about how we were raised as children easily makes parents defensive and reluctant to answer our questions. Because there is no obvious family crisis, apart from our interest in having our questions answered, our questions are likely to be thought of as uncalled for or intrusive, so they are often rejected or responded to evasively.

Questions about past events, which add information about our family histories, are usually more welcome than probing questions about family members' beliefs. When we want to know why our siblings developed strong religious beliefs, for example, we may easily be thought of as offensive rather than inquisitive, so that this line of questioning may increase families' resistance or negative reactions to our new socially intelligent ways of doing things.

Social intelligence does not encourage us to raise many questions about other family members' beliefs while we explore what social intelligence is and how it can change our lives. In this exploratory stage of becoming more aware of our social intelligence, it is usually more practical—and more socially intelligent—to gather information merely by asking ourselves the most important questions we can about why we have certain beliefs, especially if these beliefs do not seem to have constructive impacts on our lives.

For example, we benefit from raising questions around our reluctance to seriously pursue a particular career or personal relationship. We might also consider how we came to be aggressive in business relations, or passive in social exchanges. Who dominated our religious practices when we were young? Why did our parents refuse to fight in front of their children? Why did our parents always fight in front of their children? Was I an accommodating child, or difficult to deal with? Why was I so quick to anger when I was a child?

Questions like this, which gradually unearth social facts about important aspects of our beliefs, may not be answered directly by our relatives unless we find appropriate ways to raise them casually. However, we learn a great deal by trying to discern what we think our most important questions are about our beliefs. This practice prepares us for getting answers later, especially after we increase our social intelligence.

According to social intelligence principles the questions we need to raise, in order to understand more fully how we came to have our beliefs, relate particularly to our families, social classes, cultures, and societies. It may be useful to explore several sources for answers, including questioning people who are not family members—especially those who were significant influences during the formation of our beliefs. We also benefit from written sources such as family letters, historical accounts of our families, or local and national histories.

We often make these explorations alone in the first stages of understanding and changing our beliefs, so that we can be more socially intelligent in handling family reactions to our research and changed behavior. However, because family reactions can be intense and problematic, impeding our progress toward becoming more socially intelligent, they are described in greater detail below.

Family Reactions

Family members' reactions to our different ways of questioning families' beliefs and assumptions are predictably negative. The togetherness influences in families' emotional systems show that most questioning of family beliefs or family cultures is resisted, unless families are particularly open in their ways of interacting with each other. The more usual, automatic negative reactions of families to any serious questioning of their beliefs and cultures is forceful, coercive, and damaging when not dealt with appropriately by the questioner—ideally in advance of the challenges that the questions create.

Social intelligence draws attention to the power of families, as well as to their complexities. We become stronger, as well as more socially intelligent, when we are effective in dealing with our families' reactivity to what we do, or to shared life cycle events and family crises. The negativity of families' emotional systems is triggered by a variety of situations, which include questioning families' beliefs and cultures.

Social intelligence pays attention to the givens of families' emotional systems. To a certain extent modern families operate essentially as small groups which may express tribal intensities in their intergenerational loyalties. Although families' patterns of behavior vary from generation to generation, and from family to family, some characteristic reactions of families help us to understand how and why our questioning of family beliefs and cultures may evoke strong negative reactivity in our families, especially from our most dominant relatives.

When families have clear pecking orders in their hierarchies and statuses, high status family members—or family leaders—predictably set standards for how family members should respond to questions about their families' beliefs. For example, if families have specific expectations that their adult children will join family businesses, challenges to this family tradition predictably evoke strong negative reactions. In addition, many family dramas are experienced, and written up in literary forms, about the acuteness of family crises that follow in the wake of pregnancies or marriages that are disapproved of by family elders.

Social intelligence shows us that families' negative reactions to questions about family issues may create a new kind of balance or equilibrium in these families. In these situations, the thoughts and feelings of the questioning family members are usually not considered seriously. Rather, other family members form a united front to combine forces, so that they can more easily coerce the questioner who upset the status quo of their family cultures to return to how things were before these challenges.

Thus families' negative reactions to individuals who break the lockstep of families' cultural expectations express a renewed family solidarity. For example, a united front of some family members predictably opposes innovations by family members who do not do what is expected—or required—in these families' cultures.

In sum, we need to be prepared—or socially intelligent—in our efforts to neutralize the expected negative reactions of our relatives, when we try to initiate new patterns in the cultural beliefs and cultural behavior of our families. Ideally, we seek some level of agreement or understanding from our relatives in advance of our moves to do things differently, so that we earn sufficient respect from them before we try to innovate in our families. In the long run, however, we are likely to win support from our relatives, because families compromise and accommodate to each other in order to survive and thrive.

When we examine our families, beliefs, and family cultures closely, we see strong influences of interdependencies in our value choices more clearly. This knowledge allows us to avoid family dilemmas that may be triggered by making different cultural choices from our relatives. However, if we chose to move in alternative social circles, or abandon our families—at least temporarily—family issues around these cultural contrasts still need to be resolved. Cutting ourselves off from our families is an intense, negative reaction that exacts too high prices for us, our children, or our grandchildren to pay. Like it or not, our families are valuable unique lifelines to our social origins, cultural connections, and social intelligence.

From the points of view of social intelligence, changing our beliefs is important and encouraged, largely because we unwittingly absorb many unproductive or contradictory beliefs when we are children or young adults. However we should also get to know our families well enough to realize, and understand, the volatile or strong negative reactions that families often have to root changes, such as modifying basic beliefs and value choices in our families' cultures. Furthermore, social intelligence shows us that if we subject ourselves unnecessarily to families' negative reactions, we may be persuaded that living our own lives fully is not worth the effort involved. This result unfortunately discourages our endeavors to be socially intelligent in creating better cultures and societies.

Using Cultures

One of our purposes in being socially intelligent is to increase our effectiveness in accomplishing our goals. By contrast, if we conduct our lives more or less randomly, we might not formulate goals for ourselves, let alone have expectations about reaching our goals. However, when we use principles of social intelligence in our daily lives, we define goals thoughtfully and responsibly, which eventually increase the common good and social justice, as well as yield increased personal and professional satisfaction.

Social intelligence guides us to deliberately use our cultures to motivate and orient our actions in achieving our goals. For example, we deepen our understanding of our given situations by collecting social and cultural facts in the broad perspectives of families, beliefs, social classes, cultures, and societies. Then, we select values from our cultures and beliefs, so that we sustain our motivations and orientations while accomplishing our most meaningful goals to increase the common good and social justice.

Our increased objectivity, from being socially intelligent, broadens our options in using our cultures to choose new values. For example, we see more options for selecting and expressing our preferred cultural values, when our objectivity helps us to break out of the overly tight bonds of our families' cultures and beliefs. Consequently, we both understand and make use of the rich variety of value choices embodied in our families' and societies' cultures.

We also use our cultures more effectively when we study religions other than our families' religions. By understanding clusters of values and beliefs in other religions, for example, we move away from our families' cultures and establish new links with broad aspects of societies' cultures. The resonance we gain from connecting with alternative clusters of cultural values increases our freedom from our families' cultures, and increases diversity in our cultural experiences.

One of the most significant aspects of our compelling contacts with new clusters of meaningful cultural values is that our cultures become avenues of cultural and social changes. Using cultures means that we take advantage of the power of cultural symbols to create preferred cultural and social changes. For example, if we choose to change our cultures or societies, we are more successful at accomplishing this when we use the symbolic content of our families' and societies' cultures. Furthermore, we introduce new possibilities to our cultures when we make symbolic communications with local, national, and international cultures.

We are in the vanguard of formulating new meanings and new knowledge, when we use cultures to bring about cultural and social changes. Whether through formal or informal educational channels, the arts, or leisure activities, we use cultural values, beliefs, and symbols to communicate our intended changes, so that others can join us in these endeavors. Because we are socially intelligent in defining our goals, we know that we need to act collectively to accomplish what we set out to do. Working alone is too restrictive to create an effective broad outreach.

Social intelligence teaches us to recognize the power of the symbolic meanings that cultural values have in our families' cultures and beliefs, so that we can use cultures to accomplish our shared goals successfully. For example, pursuing the truth means different things to different people, depending on their particular values and beliefs. If we are successful artists, we may tend to be universalistic in our definitions and approaches to truth, which communicate meanings to broad audiences beyond local communities. If we are scientists, however, pursuing truth might require strict experimental procedures and highly specialized research goals, which are incomprehensible to many people.

Similarly the goals and roles of religious people or politicians differ, depending on the symbols they use in their communications with populations. However, each leader usually makes cultural contributions which either promote or resist changes. Because cultures need symbolic modes of communication, as well as meanings, cultural goals and beliefs are expressed differently, and have distinctive effects in contributing to the common good and social justice.

Although social intelligence is largely a pragmatic technique or methodology, it enhances our appreciation of life beyond the achievement of particular goals. Thus, our cultures should be enjoyed as well as used. However, it would be shortsighted on our parts merely to have fun in our cultures, if at the same time we close our minds to the many possibilities of using cultures to accomplish beneficial changes. We inevitably gain much shared pleasure and fulfillment through using our cultures to increase the common good and social justice.

Cultures and Fulfillment

Conventional understanding of cultures and fulfillment usually links cultures to leisure activities, or considers cultures as mere reflections of everyday life. Thus, culture is often thought of as superficial rather than in the hearts of individuals and societies. Social intelligence urges us to see cultures and fulfillment differently, so that we appreciate how our families use cultures, and the extent to which cultures inspire our beliefs and actions. From the points of view of social intelligence, culture is what we breathe in every day, so that cultures necessarily affect all our thinking and actions, as well as our fulfillment.

Given our focus on cultures in social intelligence perspectives, we need to honor some of the everyday meanings that are associated with cultures. For example, social intelligence recognizes that cultures are enjoyed in their own right in countless ways in all societies. However, social intelligence helps us not only to enjoy cultures, but to go beyond the fun and pleasure of cultures, so that we appreciate the rich varieties of cultural meanings that impact our lives. Particularly important, according to social intelligence, are the cultural influences of our families and beliefs. Our families' cultures and beliefs define significant social realities, and have strong impacts on our value choices, individual identities, and social identities.

Social intelligence views families and beliefs as important carriers of cultures, as well as important ways to understand how much we are influenced by cultures—through values, beliefs, ideas, ideals, expectations, knowledge, religions, or education. Social intelligence also sees cultures as being filtered through the five major social influences of families, beliefs, social classes, cultures, and societies. Because cultures impact themselves, they are huge masses of changing or contradictory values and beliefs, as well as cores of fairly consistent values and beliefs, which reflect societies' most agreed-on ideals and moral standards.

One of the emphases of social intelligence, in interpreting cultural and social facts, is that cultures initiate changes in social processes, due to the impacts of value choices on individual or social priorities and goals. Social intelligence—particularly our awareness of social influences—guides us to make more effective, consequential changes in societies through our value choices.

Our value choices enable us to express ourselves constructively through our contributions to the common good and social justice, which bring considerable satisfaction and fulfillment. In fact, when we are committed to increasing our social intelligence, it is often difficult for us to continue to gain as much satisfaction and fulfillment from conventional pleasure-seeking, as from being historical actors who contribute to the common good and social justice.

Social intelligence gives us pointers on how to understand social influences more fully—particularly the social influences of families, beliefs, social classes, cultures, and societies—so that we make value choices to increase our social intelligence and enhance our contributions to the common good and social justice. When we know that we are on this track, and that we are headed in constructive directions, we gain satisfaction and fulfillment. We realize that we are doing whatever we can to bring about better futures. Furthermore, although we may not achieve our goals, aiming to increase social justice makes substantial qualitative differences to our appreciation of ourselves, others, our communities, our societies, and globalization.

Our value choices make this sequence of events both possible and probable. Choosing constructive, collectivity-oriented, life-directed values, for example, enlightens our actions, increases the beneficial impacts of our actions, and sustains our fulfillment. From the points of view of social intelligence, knowing social facts grounds our actions in practical strategies that support cooperation with others. This increases our effectiveness and fulfillment as agents of cultural and social change.

Social intelligence suggests that education may also turn us around from our mundane, everyday worlds, so that we face—and deal with—broad cultural issues about our survival and fulfillment. Although we learn a great deal from appreciating the crisis dimensions of our current cultural situations, we also indisputably benefit from understanding local and global cultural histories, or from recognizing repeated patterns in diverse cultures. Thus, education and learning expand our horizons, and integrate the broad perspectives of social intelligence more meaningfully and more purposefully. For example, we increase our fulfillment when we use our socially intelligent knowledge about cultures to improve our societies and strengthen social justice.

VIII. Social Classes and Societies

To the extent that modern societies have more complex social classes than historic or preliterate societies, cultures have overlapping boundaries that reflect continuing increases in the number of different social class bases. For example, although today's social classes are still divided according to social connections among individuals and families, or their material assets, social classes are now also based on race, ethnicity, gender, sexual orientation, religion, education, age, and health or ablebodiedness.

As social class bases multiply, cultures diversify to represent the distinctive values and beliefs of members of different social classes. Sometimes the value differences within and among social class cultures are harmonious—perhaps because they appear to be complementary in the short run—but ultimately social class cultures inevitably magnify the intensity and competitiveness of conflicting social class interests.

Social intelligence teaches us to be aware of social class differences in opportunities and their impacts on our cultures and societies. For example, social class cultures not only express social class tensions, but they also exacerbate them. Furthermore, because of the relatively recent occurrence of diversified social class cultures, the potential for new social class conflicts endures. Social intelligence teaches us that we need to be aware of how our cultures are influenced by the power that members of different social classes have or do not have, particularly because members of upper social classes often use their cultural power and resources to exploit or oppress members of lower social classes.

Because social intelligence views religions and education as significant dimensions of cultures, special attention is given to ways in which religions and education serve as social class bases which maintain the status quo, or bring about cultural and social changes. For example, although it is clear that many contemporary societies have enhanced their cultures due to mass education, it is largely upper social class privileges that are reinforced by advanced education. Thus, education is a gateway to cultural refinements that often ensure upper social class membership rather than basic principles of equality.

Religions are often related to social class concerns in less obvious or less critical ways than education. However, religions also often inspire deep motivations to change social conditions by rebelling against unjust social and cultural privileges, or by appealing to supernatural forces to bring about social revolutions for social justice. Thus the consequences of individual and social identifications with religions are of considerable importance to both cultures and societies.

Because social intelligence shows that cultures may bring about deep levels of social change, we know that our personal and social value choices influence our individual and social wellbeing. For example, when we change our input in cultural and social processes, cultural and social outcomes automatically change. This reciprocity between our cultures and societies may inspire us to design alternatives to social classes, especially in light of the strife and restrictions that characterize social class hierarchies in current societies.

The principles of social intelligence help us to discern how our families, beliefs and cultures affect our social classes or societies and vice versa. Historically, social classes have been viewed as important catalysts in broad social changes such as the industrial revolution. In recent years, however, cultures are also associated with the industrial revolution. For example, there is increasing acceptance of the social fact that cultures are significant determinants of social and economic conditions in societies as well as social classes.

Social intelligence encourages us to be objective about cultures, social classes, and societies by paying close attention to the social facts that result from these influences. Social intelligence also suggests that if we want to design strategies for interventions and social changes these should be grounded in social facts, in order to be socially intelligent. For example, we need to be as objective as possible in these endeavors, so that we guard and preserve the freedom necessary to create beneficial cultural and social changes.

Because of the breadth of cultures, social classes, and societies we must balance our assessments of past, present, and future social conditions at the same time that we design strategies and blueprints for changes. For example, cultures are often associated with traditions of the past, but traditions also continue and can be modified—to some extent—in today's societies.

Although traditions lose power in modern societies, they may be extremely influential in resisting cultural and social changes, especially when family cultures and family beliefs are based on traditions. In any event, we need to clarify our perspectives on the past in relation to needs of the present and future, so that we understand and work strategically with our cultures and societies.

Social Classes Diversify Cultures

The cultures of social classes often reinforce classes' separateness from each other, as well as specific contrasts among classes. By definition, social classes have distinctive vested interests, which are reflected in characteristics of their different bases. Social intelligence encourages us to be increasingly aware of the substance of social class distinctions, and of the many impacts that our omnipresent social classes have on our lives.

For example, we think, feel, and act in response to our social class situations and social class cultures. Therefore, cultural differences among social classes reinforce opportunity structures and varied lifestyles. If we want to be upwardly socially mobile, even though we may accumulate the economic resources necessary, we must also learn different ways to present and conduct ourselves in public in order to meet social class cultural expectations for membership in our new social classes.

Social intelligence encourages us to become researchers of social classes, so that we do not align our personal goals too closely with social class goals. Although social classes are constantly recruiting individuals and families, we need to be detached and objective about social class processes if we are to be socially intelligent. For example, social intelligence requires us to contribute to the common good, rather than to be socially mobile through following social class dictates for success.

As social classes become more subtle in modern societies— in part due to higher levels of education, better standards of living, and the overall consumer patterns needed for capitalist profits—social classes reflect differences in races, ethnicity, education, religion, gender, sexual orientation, age, and health or ablebodiedness. Historic social class criteria of social connections and material assets also continue to reinforce social class differences in modern societies, often having different outcomes than other social class bases. Ultimately, however, overlapping social class criteria prevent easy or clear social class demarcations, so that ambiguities inevitably accompany social class rankings in modern cultures and societies.

This increased complexity in defining social classes does not make the multiple social class hierarchies of modern societies any less significant than social classes in more traditional societies. For example, in modern societies we often give much thought to our physical appearance and leisure habits, as well as to how we earn our incomes. Thus, our more diversified social classes continue to have strong impacts on our cultures and societies.

When we want to relate to others, by making them special in our lives, we usually learn about their cultures and participate in these cultures whenever possible. In an interfaith intermarriage, for example, one partner may convert to the other's religion, in part to respect and honor that person. Because cultures are learned, we frequently choose to learn others' cultures.

Consequently, and also because cultures are acquired, social intelligence encourages us to learn whatever we need to know in order to be effective independent agents within and among cultures and societies.

Social intelligence reminds us that if we want to promote peaceful coexistence among societies, learning about others' cultures is crucial. For example, however difficult it may be to learn different cultures, it is easier and more practical to do this than to deal with class conflicts exacerbated by diminishing the importance of others' cultures. Moreover, we often express our hatred of others by refusing to learn about their cultures, or by destroying their cultures.

At best, cultures suggest directions for social change and peaceful coexistence. Although this is not all that cultures do, these are some of the most significant outcomes of cultural interventions. When we respect others' cultures we demonstrate that the world can be a better place, and that our best cultural and value choices move us toward more fulfilling futures. Therefore, we can usefully invest our socially intelligent hopes in cultures as sources of cultural, moral, and social ideals for all societies and civilizations.

To a certain extent cultures also diversify social classes. For example, the more recent social class bases—race, ethnicity, gender, sexual orientation, education, religion, health and ablebodiedness—derive from cultural sources, or from cultural expressions of material and physiological conditions. Furthermore, because all social classes have cultural aspects, cultural definitions and cultural divisions among social classes are powerful indicators of social status. In these respects, the cultural criteria of contemporary social classes may outweigh the strategic significance of the more backward-looking traditional social and economic bases of social classes.

Class Conflicts in Cultures

Social intelligence suggests that many cultural contrasts among social classes cause, or result from, historical and contemporary social class conflicts. For example, we use societal or historical perspectives to understand clashes in social class cultures of the past. Here social facts show us not only the pervasiveness of social class cultures in societies, but also the political tensions that existed—and still exist—between upper and lower social class cultures.

Because social class culture conflicts may eventually lead to civil wars or international wars, they need to be recognized for their destructive potential. However, to the extent that we deliberately use social intelligence principles to make our social class cultures less oppositional, for example, we can neutralize some of the most extreme tensions in these conflicts, thereby protecting the populations involved. Thus, although social class cultures sometimes escalate political polarities, social class cultures may also enhance peaceful purposes, especially when we deliberately preserve freedom and increase the common good. However, when economic or political interests prevail in social class culture conflicts, peaceful coexistence is usually difficult or impossible to accomplish.

Social intelligence allows us to identify not only extreme forms of class conflicts in our cultures and societies, but also some of the most significant ways in which our social class cultures divide societies and cultivate meaningless competitiveness. For example, when we consider social class cultures based on sexual orientations, we see patterns of values in heterosexual and homosexual cultures that polarize and exaggerate cultural differences between these two social classes. Consequently, competitiveness for individual and social rights—around the issue of sexual orientations—is heightened as well as political tensions.

Social intelligence suggests that we should recognize qualitative characteristics of social class cultures as vital ways to express creative cultural differences. In the long run, however, we need to find practical ways to develop social conditions that promote peaceful coexistence among social classes and their cultures, rather than encourage extreme competitiveness and conflicts. When we cooperate with each other rather than compete, for example, we establish stable and effective ways to do things, at the same time that we ensure standards that support tolerance among social classes and their cultures.

If we want to increase our social intelligence, tensions between social class cultures based on heterosexual and homosexual orientations, may become a focus for our community contributions to strengthen the common good and social justice. We may work to improve communications between these two social classes, for example, or apply socially intelligent strategies to reduce prejudice, discrimination, and other unfair practices. Furthermore, when we draw attention to social injustices about sexual orientation classes, populations understand more fully that we cannot afford to exclude any social classes from the benefits of societies or globalization.

Social class cultures not only express themselves as social classes, or as symbolic social arrangements in our societies, but also as social contexts. For example, in order to assure tolerance and welcoming responses to both heterosexual and homosexual cultural differences, we need to examine social class cultures in our families and beliefs. This is important because our families and beliefs are foundations of our social class affiliations and identifications. Social histories of social classes show that social classes are supported by tenacious cultures of competitiveness, which in part derive from our families, beliefs, and sexual orientations.

One way to change the divisiveness and destructiveness of social class cultures is to use social intelligence to design different ways to organize our populations, so that social class conflicts do not dominate social class cultures and societal cultures. For example, when we single out and honor particular values—such as equality—that we prefer as foundations for more cooperative societies, we gradually cooperate more effectively with others to build better futures.

Social intelligence suggests that making value choices to prioritize equality, inclusiveness, diversity, cooperation, and openness increases the common good and social justice. These new cultures eventually replace some of the harmful competitiveness of current social class cultures, by neutralizing or eliminating their most destructive characteristics. Thus, the values of equality, inclusiveness, diversity, cooperation, and openness establish cultural and social conditions that increase the likelihood that social classes are replaced by effective and meaningful new ways to organize our populations.

Above all we look to social intelligence principles to guide us in these difficult, sometimes impossible cultural tasks. We are emboldened sufficiently by socially intelligent knowledge to assume lifetime tasks which cannot be completed, but rather carried forward from generation to generation. We are here to work decisively toward improving cultural and social conditions in societies now, so that we live more fully and more justly while creating better futures. Furthermore, we know that we need to stay committed to these tasks if we are to honor social intelligence and social justice in our ongoing cultures and societies.

Cultural Solutions to Classes?

When we use social intelligence to recognize the importance of social class cultures in maintaining social classes and bringing about cultural and social changes, we consider the extent to which changing our social class cultures resolves social class problems. Beyond the social class culture conflicts that we have already considered in the previous subsection of *Cultures and Social Intelligence*, we turn our attention to the social inequalities that social classes and social class cultures create or sustain, and the relationship of social class cultures and societal cultures to these inequalities.

One of the pernicious consequences of social classes and social class cultures is that they accentuate economic and power contrasts between members of upper and lower social classes. For example, in many industrial societies modernization widened gaps between the rich and poor, rather than narrowed extremes in social class differences. These social facts are important to ponder, because they may have disastrous implications for people who are poor and unable to represent their own interests directly in crucial political decision-making.

For example, social facts document the harsh realities of poverty, and the inadequate resources of members of lower social classes in both poor and prosperous societies. Therefore, our most important questions must address how we can provide sufficient goods and services to people in need, rather than merely assess the many dimensions of poverty in poor economic conditions.

Social intelligence emphasizes that social classes have persisted through time largely because social and political vested interests are supported by maintaining social, economic, and political inequalities. Therefore, we need to answer questions such as whose interests are met and unmet by social class cultures? What practical things can we do to change these social injustices? How can social intelligence guide us to make sufficient constructive changes in social class cultures to redesign the status quo?

First, social intelligence suggests that in order to change social class cultures, we should address members of upper social classes—that is, those who have sufficient material and educational resources—so that we can more easily make real differences in present social class cultures. For example, we use social intelligence principles to inspire members of upper social classes to become more responsible for others' well-being, so that financial resources may be redistributed to reduce alienation in societies. When members of upper social classes redefine their responsibilities to include changing social class cultures and societies, it is more likely that other social class cultures and societies will change.

For example, aiming to change the cultures of upper social classes, so that upper social class members identify injustices in their social class privileges, is a constructive step to improve conditions in lower social classes. Also, educating upper social class members so that they increase their responsibilities for changing social class cultures and social classes, shows us how changing social class cultures can solve some problems in societies. Although making different value choices in lower social class cultures is also important, especially in the long run, changing value choices in upper social class cultures may be more influential in narrowing gaps between the wealthy and the poor in contemporary affluent societies.

Societies often resist making policies explicitly to change social classes, which is one reason why cultural means of change need to be seriously considered. For example, when sufficient people in societies make value choices that support equality, inclusiveness, diversity, cooperation, and openness, a critical mass of people in societies will gradually establish momentums for social changes. These changed values are crucial for bringing about constructive social changes, because cultures and social classes are essential components in organizing societies.

One of the conclusions we draw from using social intelligence principles to solve problems related to social class cultures, is that social intelligence is an effective problem-solving technique. For example, when we examine our individual and social situations from the points of view of social intelligence, we maintain the broad perspectives of families, beliefs, social classes, cultures, and societies in order to understand and solve our problems effectively. Furthermore, when we increase our social intelligence, the common good, and social justice—as well as move toward establishing equality, inclusiveness, diversity, cooperation, and openness through making different value choices—we are more creative in discovering new ways to do whatever is needed to improve our futures.

Societies in Cultures

Societies are reflected in their cultures in many different ways. For example, when people speak the same languages and use the same national symbols, they communicate effectively with each other and create artistic works that express their individualities as members of societies with shared national or international interests. The dominant cultures of societies are expressed in national and international dialogues that help us to clarify and understand the main social and historical issues of our day.

Thus cultures essentially define our nations' priorities. It is difficult to think outside our cultures, so we are often identified through cultural boundaries in what we say, how we say it, and what we do. Cultures include ways of accomplishing goals in particular societies, and some historical traditions continue to influence what we do in specific situations.

Most modern societies have cultures that reflect different social classes, with the result that different social class cultures have specific perspectives on societies. For example, dominant mainstream upper middle class cultures often revere their own societies by focusing on maintaining them. By contrast, less powerful lower class cultures often oppose the dominant cultures of their societies. Therefore, depending on the viewpoint of the social class culture with which a person or group identifies, societies may be praised or vilified and upheld or diminished by social class cultures.

Social intelligence increases our objectivity, so that we make more accurate assessments of varied cultural interpretations of societies. Because we have to decide which cultural perspectives are closest to the social realities we believe in, social intelligence helps us to select cultural views of societies that we find most meaningful and helpful. For example, we may use religious perspectives on societies in our assessments, or different genders' views of societies.

Establishing a reliable world view is an advantageous cultural venture whether we realize this or not. Even though we may feel that we stand on shifting sands when we make our most significant value choices, these are important shifting sands and they may be all we have to gauge our actions in difficult circumstances. We cannot escape the social fact that we need cultural filters to examine our societies and assess them. Moreover, our most critical choices lie in deciding which values we select to give us dependable pointers for achieving meaningful world views, social actions, and goals.

Cultures are important not only because cultures change cultures and societies, but because our cultures define our societies. For example, we cannot see our societies clearly without cultural prisms, so that our views of our own and other societies ultimately depend on our cultural values and beliefs.

Our values and beliefs are essential building blocks of who we are, who we want to be, what we want to accomplish, and what our societies are. We necessarily view ourselves in relation to others in our societies, and we determine what we want to accomplish when we understand the social and cultural dimensions of our talents and accomplishments more fully.

After we clarify our national identities through our cultures, value choices, and beliefs, we understand more clearly what it means to be a member of the world community. We do not lose our national identities in this process, even though we may assume additional characteristics of national identities in response to foreigners' expectations for us as members of our societies or the world community. Although we also deviate from others' views of us, they inevitably impact the substance of our national or international communications and interactions.

Social intelligence encourages us to deliberately immerse ourselves in our cultures, so that we stay current in our understanding of societies and communications. Being immersed in cultures allows us to draw on fresh cultural resources that strengthen our capacities to understand ourselves and others, so that we make more effective contributions to the common good and social justice. However, we may not choose to challenge our societies in times of war, for example, because it could be more strategic to conform during political and economic crises.

We get to know other societies by understanding their cultures. For example, we experience some societies' cultural habits and rituals by eating their foods or celebrating their national holidays. We may do this deliberately to identify more closely with unfamiliar societies, so that we understand them more fully. Furthermore, because other societies and cultures are expressed in everything their people do, their cultures deepen our understanding of their values.

Cultures in Societies

In their first stages of development, single coherent cultures bind their communities and societies. Through time, whether many or few cultures exist in societies today, cultures often maintain fairly distinctive local or national boundaries. However, cultures have become more mobile and versatile because of globalization. For example, cultures migrate, are imported by other countries, or accommodate to other societies' cultures. Ultimately, because societies often create a more cohesive world community through globalization—largely due to the underlying world economy—the world system of societies includes national and international cultures in the same way that national cultures were formerly composed of different local cultures.

Social intelligence pays attention to historical trends in the development of complex international and global cultures, as well as the ways in which common denominators in cultures emerge. For example, complex cultures often reflect the hegemony of the most powerful societies in the world economy or world politics. Social intelligence helps us to understand the power and complexities of these cultures and societies. Furthermore, social intelligence emphasizes that each of us is directly related to these global processes, so we can at least indirectly influence cultural and social global changes through our value choices.

Because social intelligence helps us to see connections between our personal lives, cultures, and globalization, we need not become passive pawns in the power and complexities of cultural and social changes. Rather we assume responsibilities as active participants who make differences in the present and future outcomes of globalization. For example, when we are socially intelligent, we understand how global cultures impact our everyday lives, so that our decisions and commitments inspire actions that have significant cultural and social results.

The trajectories we follow, when we are guided by social intelligence principles, heighten our awareness of social and cultural influences. We examine the five strongest cultural and social influences of families, beliefs, social classes, cultures, and societies, so that we can commit ourselves more fully as responsible historical actors. Furthermore, we choose to increase our social intelligence, as well as the common good and social justice, by making cultural choices that emphasize constructive values and beliefs—such as equality, inclusiveness, diversity, cooperation, and openness.

This is how we come to understand the power and complexities of cultures in our personal lives and societies. Consequently, we make more thoughtful decisions about how we contribute to cultures in our everyday behavior. We bear in mind, according to the principles of social intelligence, that there is no escape from our cultures and their influences. We cannot choose not to make value choices, decisions, or commitments, because these are vital aspects of being alive in our societies. Therefore, when we put social intelligence to its best uses, we make value choices about cultures that enhance our families, communities, societies, civilizations, and the global community.

Even though our cultures are restricted to some extent by our societies or globalization, they are also somewhat free from these influences. For example, national and global boundaries cannot limit information and knowledge indefinitely. People are hungry for knowledge and know-how to meet their existential needs to survive and be fulfilled. In these respects, cultures often travel freely from society to society—especially when societies are open—so that national cultures enter directly into social exchanges that create global cultures.

Cultures are masses of harmonious and contradictory symbols, which have varied meanings for populations in the same and different societies. However, there are also strong universalistic elements in cultures, because we all inhabit planet earth. For example, we want as many people and societies as possible to survive and be fulfilled.

Social intelligence is a pragmatic strategy that helps us to reach goals that improve our cultures, societies, and civilizations constructively. When we use our hearts and minds to their fullest capacities, we take charge of our destinies, and protect those who cannot help themselves. This expresses the spirit of social intelligence in our cultures and societies.

As participants in cultures, we wield some power over how societies are. For example, new ideas, designs, and inventions open up our societies, and make more meaningful and more productive communications possible. Because cultures are vital to our societies and globalization, cultural exchanges among societies make wide varieties of constructive cultural and societal accomplishments possible.

Cultural and Social Changes

In the normal course of events, cultural and social changes happen. In fact, we cannot escape the impacts of cultural and social changes, however much we may try. For example, modern technologies exist in the furthest outreaches of the world today, so that even traveling to distant places may no longer cut us off from civilizations. Furthermore, wherever we go, we necessarily carry images or tools of our civilizations with us.

Some of the cultural and social changes that happen, without much awareness of individuals and populations, are slow gradual changes in international development or evolution. For example, communications—through travel or electronic means—open up possibilities for the diffusion of cultures among societies. Also, when we are young, we are relatively passive beneficiaries of varied social class cultural heritages, some of which are bought— as consumer goods—by our families.

Social intelligence makes us more aware of the cultural and social class processes that culminate in social changes. Social intelligence also invites us to see cultural and social class changes as avenues for participation in these changes. By concentrating on major social influences and crucial value choices, social intelligence makes it clear that we become more effective agents of change when we increase our social intelligence, and live deliberately as historical actors.

Social intelligence stresses the importance of learning social facts, in order to grasp the power and complexities of the major social influences of families, beliefs, social classes, cultures, and societies. Furthermore, we learn how to be more objective in our assessments of these influences, and their impacts on our lives. These accomplishments give us increased control over social and cultural situations, as well as our personal lives, particularly by making specific value choices and commitments to accomplish cultural or social changes.

Although some social changes seem to occur independently, rather than as results of cultural influences—such as people's decisions to have children or experts' scientific discoveries—when we examine patterns of behavior and sequences of events more closely, we often find that cultural conditions influenced these outcomes. Moreover, we still tend to think of our cultures as arenas of entertainment or artistic accomplishment, rather than pay attention to the omnipresence of cultures and cultural changes.

Social intelligence implies that cultures change societies. Social intelligence also acknowledges, however, that material resources may bring about cultural and social changes, as well as political power. Realistically cultures, material resources, and political power are often interdependent means of bringing about cultural and social changes.

One of the ways in which cultures are particularly significant agents of social changes is that cultures express everyday realities. We have access to cultures at every point of our daily lives because we eat, sleep, and breathe cultures, as well as exchange ideas in cultural terms and cultural contexts.

This means that not only is culture a significant way and power to change cultures and societies, but it is also within the reaches and experiences of most people. Cultures seep into the hearts and minds of all, regardless of whether we decide to use cultures for broader purposes. Although we inevitably use cultures in our exchanges with others, we cannot control cultural outcomes until we make more selective and more deliberate uses of our value choices and other cultural resources.

One of the later stages of being socially intelligent is to make decisions to work toward social justice, which can be thought of as a moral ideal, a value, or a culture in its own right. Working together with others to increase social justice is a particularly vital and effective aspect of changing our cultures, because we necessarily accomplish more when we work with others than when we work alone. Because social justice is sometimes associated with the constructive value choices of equality, inclusiveness, diversity, cooperation, and openness, social justice is a powerful direction in which cultures and societies move, especially to accomplish better futures.

It is not that we need to actually increase social justice in order to be assured that our futures will be better than the present, but rather that we accept the constructive values of social justice as cultural orientations for our actions, so that we move in these directions as decisively as possible. Because our lives are essentially unfinished journeys, we live fully when we merely try to accomplish what we believe in the most, and leave cultural legacies that benefit others.

IX. Social Justice

Social intelligence is not initially, or even ultimately, directly related to social justice. Rather, social intelligence is a way of looking at the world, a tool for social change, an enhancement of meanings in everyday life, and a social skill based on social facts and objectivity. Social intelligence is also a means to accomplish deliberately chosen goals effectively.

Social justice comes into focus as we develop and increase our social intelligence, because we question more deeply what the purposes of being alive and having socially intelligent know-how are. For example, how can we share our knowledge of social intelligence? As with any other aspect of social living, moral purposes cannot be pushed away indefinitely because moral issues enter into our existential mandate to live fully. Social intelligence recognizes this social fact, and helps us to make sense of these issues in our everyday situations.

First, social intelligence is initially concerned with an awakening process, which focuses on recognizing the power and complexities of the five social influences of families, beliefs, social classes, cultures, and societies. Although others may see social influences differently, a strong case can be made that families, beliefs, social classes, cultures, and societies affect individuals, families, groups, communities, societies, civilizations, and globalization so deeply that they predispose us to act constructively or destructively.

Next, social intelligence requires us to use our knowledge of social influences to maintain broad social perspectives, increase objectivity, and bring about social changes informed by social facts. For example, we apply social intelligence to ourselves by reviewing social facts that show us how families, beliefs, social classes, cultures, and societies have affected our lives, current behavior, and goals. We then make changes in our families, beliefs, social classes, cultures, and societies depending on how we understand these influences in our lives, and how we think we can make significant differences in societies for the present and future.

Only when we have sufficient social intelligence and constructive engagement in major social processes, are we ready to consider social justice issues objectively, as well as incorporate social justice in our lives. We then pay close attention to the implications of social justice and how we can be more responsible with regard to social justice, particularly by working with others to achieve similar social justice goals.

Ideally, we do not plunge into social justice work before this time in our development as historical actors, because social intelligence and social justice are not synonymous. We need a heightened awareness of the impacts of social influences, as well as mature social intelligence, before we can understand social justice sufficiently to make thoughtful commitments to increase social justice effectively.

Thus, social justice is a direction in which to apply social intelligence principles. The definitions, descriptions, and explanations of social intelligence in *Cultures and Social Intelligence* are intentionally biased in favor of recognizing social intelligence as a vital aspect of accomplishing constructive rather than destructive purposes. Unfortunately, however, both historically and in contemporary times, social intelligence is used for destructive as well as constructive purposes. Nevertheless, in light of the spirit of *Cultures and Social Intelligence*, the emphasis on social justice here is that social justice is one of the most significant moral and practical goals toward which we can aim, through applying purposeful, socially intelligent actions.

Social justice is therefore a cultural ideal that motivates us to nurture particular cultural values and value choices. In these respects social justice is a powerful cultural and social influence, as well as a basis for commitments and strategies to increase the common good. Even though social justice may not appear to affect everyone in populations directly—as do the social influences of families, beliefs, social classes, cultures, and societies—social justice is an ethical and moral possibility that we can actualize, especially in social problem-solving ventures. For example, we use social justice to motivate us to design and initiate cultural and social changes, so that we create a more livable present and future for more people.

Ideally we initiate social justice actions, as well as make social justice commitments, when we are sufficiently socially intelligent to be responsible historical actors. Although everyone is an historical actor—just as everyone has some degree of social intelligence—deliberately increasing our social intelligence gives us a fuller realization of how vocations or missions develop from our capacities to be more socially intelligent. For example, we readily choose to make the world better rather than worse, with respect to global human rights to survive and be fulfilled. By using the broad perspectives of social intelligence, together with our enhanced capacities to understand social issues and apply social intelligence principles, we commit some purposes and directions of our lives to increasing the common good and social justice.

Our deeper understanding of social justice and social intelligence encourages us to assume more responsibilities as historical actors, because we are interested in making deliberate efforts to express constructive value choices—such as equality, inclusiveness, diversity, cooperation, and openness—in our everyday lives. Although this is not an exhaustive list of constructive social or moral values, these value choices illustrate how social intelligence can be brought to fruition through continuing to increase social intelligence, the common good, and social justice.

Historical Actors

From the points of view of social intelligence, history is a perspective on time and societies that gives us information about trends in events that produce patterns in cultural and social changes. Histories vary, depending on the contexts in which time and social changes are recorded, measured, and interpreted. For example, histories may be based on families, cultures, communities, local regions, nations, international relations, or globalization. Each of these historical perspectives emphasizes particular events and uses different time frames, showing us that human behavior is affected directly by both local and global social influences.

Historical actors include people who live in various time periods and contrasting social contexts, including the present. We are historical actors by virtue of being alive. Even if we are deliberately passive in our behavior and actions, we are historical actors because we exist. However, people do not usually consider themselves as historical actors, especially if they think that they have few or no impacts on history or social situations. By contrast, social intelligence teaches us that feeling powerless is often directly related to problematic social conditions. When we become more active in our responses to our social situations, we help ourselves and others to take charge of our lives and destinies.

For example, to the extent that we see ourselves as having meaning or purpose, we understand that what we do makes differences in the complex mass of interactions we enter into each day. This socially intelligent awareness suggests that we are historical actors, and social intelligence helps us to nurture social purposes, so that we gradually become more intentioned historical actors who increase the common good and social justice.

We continue to increase our social intelligence when we are historical actors, by recognizing that we are learning how to be the historical actors that we already are. For example, we learn more about the cultural options and value choices we can express as historical actors at the same time that we increase the effectiveness of our socially intelligent actions.

Social justice gives us a moral compass for applying social intelligence in our everyday lives. Although historical actors frequently assume leadership responsibilities to bring their goals to fruition, this is not a necessary consequence of becoming an aware historical actor. For example, we may decide to be more subtle in our missions as historical actors, so that we are less identifiable in what we accomplish. When we decide to increase the common good, we automatically increase our social intelligence as responsible historical actors.

Cultures give us moral purposes as historical actors through their languages, values, ideals, beliefs, meanings, knowledge, religions, legal systems, norms, standards, and ways of doing things. Cultures include leadership styles as well as lifestyles and symbolic communications. Cultures also guide our socially intelligent goals, so that we engage in actions with like-minded others more effectively, to accomplish whatever goals we think are important. For example, as historical actors we make decisions to achieve goals that are based on our most cherished value choices and cultural preferences.

Socially intelligent historical actors are more deliberate in making value choices and expressing cultural preferences in their actions than other people. For example, they choose to use ranges of constructive value choices—such as equality, inclusiveness, diversity, cooperation, and openness—in their work and commitments, or single out one particular value choice to motivate and orient their actions, such as equality. Socially intelligent historical actors also work with others who make similar value choices, and who orient their actions to the future as well as the present.

If historical actors are habituated to working alone in their accomplishments, social intelligence shows them how to be more effective by working with those who have similar purposes. We are not as productive as historical actors when we work in isolation, largely because we need a free flow of cultural ideas and diverse actions in our work in order to increase the common good. We need to give away our socially intelligent knowledge to others, and cooperation inspires us to think more carefully about social justice issues as well as what we want to accomplish.

When we are responsible historical actors we stay in touch with social facts in whatever we set out to accomplish and with whomever we work. Some of these social facts are historical, because it is essential that as historical actors we are aware of the nature of our changing times and changing cultures as we go about our business. In this way cultural and social patterns continue to guide historical actors to increase the common good and social justice. This allows us to keep our fingers on the pulses of cultural and social life as they are lived in the present, in order to influence our futures meaningfully.

Equality

Equality is one of the most significant values and value choices frequently associated with the cultural ideal of social justice. Although some people may prefer to be motivated and oriented by values and value choices other than social justice and equality—at the same time that they increase their social intelligence and the common good as historical actors—equality is an example of a worthwhile socially intelligent value and value choice that has constructive social consequences for cultures, societies, and globalization.

Using the value of equality to guide our thinking, in addition to the principles of social intelligence, helps us to discover circumstances and issues related to equality in our families, beliefs, social classes, cultures, and societies. For example, when we consider our families' histories, we often find that family traditions—like respecting family elders—may or may not have continued to the present day. Also, because Western societies' cultural attitudes toward family elders show decreased respect during the nineteenth and twentieth centuries, many elders are not treated as equals—even though in a more remote past they may have received more than their fair share of attention and support from other family members.

Similarly, we need to examine our child-rearing practices. For example, modern cultures often encourage middle class families to focus on child care—by giving their children varied educational benefits—with the result that many privileged children receive more goods and services than they need for their health and well-being. When this dynamic occurs in families' emotional systems, some family members' needs may be put on hold or ignored, in order to push children to excel or achieve their parents' goals.

Furthermore, traditional gender roles are often perpetuated in modern families, even though some of the terms of spouses' relationships seem to be current with respect to twenty first century Western social ideals. For instance, when men continue to be privileged through family support, especially due to their spouses' domestic labor, gender inequities continue to be expressed in the present generations of families. In order to achieve equality, both women and men need to express the cultural value of equality through their daily decisions and actions. If they merely conduct business as usual, they tend to perpetuate unequal social advantages for men.

In addition to formulating broad views of inequalities in our families, social intelligence encourages us consider what equal conditions in our families look like. For example, we need to think through how using a social intelligence principle of balance in personal relationships and families' emotional systems would increase equality in our families. Focusing on equality not only creates a standard for us to assess what is really going on in our families, but it also directs us toward creating more constructively balanced relationships in our families in the present for the future.

Similarly, we benefit from examining our beliefs and assumptions about equality by looking at how we conduct our daily lives, particularly by considering our beliefs and assumptions about the equality of those with whom we interact the most. Emotional climates are contagious, for example, so we inevitably find it difficult to take stands on the significance of the cultural value of equality in social relations when the groups we belong to resist or are impervious to concerns about equality. Social intelligence suggests that we are more likely to accomplish our goals to increase equality when we associate with those who accept equality as a primary organizing principle.

In addition to examining the impact—or lack of impact—of equality in our families and beliefs, we benefit from identifying similar concerns in our social classes, cultures, and societies. For example, we come to realize that the hierarchical structures of our social classes are founded on assumptions and values related to privileging inequalities in order to make our social classes viable. Furthermore, when we realize the destructiveness of the social consequences that social classes bring to members of lower classes, we see urgent needs that value choices achieve equality rather than inequality in our cultures and societies.

Examinations of inequality and equality in our cultures and societies also draw attention to the depth and seriousness of social problems that result from inequalities. For example, we realize that we face many challenges in bringing equality—as an organizing principle—into societal arenas. Moreover, when we consider equality in globalization, we see that we must equalize tasks and their rewards from generation to generation to produce improved futures.

Inclusiveness

Inclusiveness is a second significant value and value choice that is often associated with the cultural ideals of equality and social justice because inclusiveness focuses on considering all members of populations. Like equality, inclusiveness is an example of a worthwhile socially intelligent value and value choice that has constructive social consequences for social justice in societies and globalization. Furthermore, inclusiveness can be considered as a single constructive value for motivating and orienting our behavior, or as one of a cluster of related constructive values and value choices.

Inclusiveness emphasizes universality in our thoughts and actions about individual and social privileges. For example, inclusiveness suggests that we have rights as members of particular societies or as human beings. We also need to be respected and treated as significant participants in our families, communities, societies, and globalization. Thus, inclusiveness means that we should be able to belong fully to the most central groups and organizations in our societies, or to have access to our societies' social and cultural privileges.

History shows us that specific racial, ethnic, gender, and age groups have been excluded from the social benefits of inclusiveness because of prejudice and discrimination. Sometimes the social and cultural practices that support exclusivity are institutionalized—even within our religions and legal systems—with the result that it is very difficult to make sufficient inroads to reform behavior that does not express the cultural value of inclusiveness.

In spite of these problematic historical precedents, where exclusivity rather than inclusiveness has been upheld, social intelligence teaches us that because prejudice and discrimination are learned, these destructive practices can be unlearned, reformed, and replaced. For example, we can invent or design more inclusive ways to organize our societies, as well as more effective means to create new traditions of inclusiveness.

Although there are overlaps between the cultural values of equality and inclusiveness, the emphases given by each of these values are sufficiently different to separate some of their social consequences. For example, whereas equality goes to the heart of the nature of human nature and traditional understandings about being equal children of God, inclusiveness is a standard for conducting our everyday lives as individuals, historical actors, communities, and societies.

In making these distinctions, we ask ourselves to what extent human nature drives us to be tribal in our orientations to our families, communities, and other social groups, so that we put our own groups before other groups by restricting interactions with them. For example, exclusive patterns of behavior are found throughout history—in preliterate societies as well as modern societies. When we use social intelligence to learn more about ourselves and our societies, we realize that what we do creates social conditions for both our present and future societies. Consequently, we need to be inclusive in our actions, so that everyone can ultimately have opportunities to benefit from social mobility and social resources. These are practical applications, implications, and results of expressing the cultural value of inclusiveness in our current value choices.

Because social intelligence principles uphold necessities to honor inclusiveness for our long term survival and fulfillment, we must decide how to organize our populations most effectively. Social intelligence reinforces the view that because we have choices, we can learn how to do things differently. For example, rather than repeat behavior that we mistakenly believe is human nature, or ruminate endlessly about how difficult it is to counteract particular human tendencies, social intelligence suggests that we make different value choices such as honoring inclusiveness.

Even though we may believe that social policies that support inclusiveness in modern societies go against human nature, we can perhaps accept the principle that our societies and civilizations need to create social conditions that make peaceful coexistence possible. When we open up our exclusive groups, we increase benefits for more people, and are more likely to develop opportunities for all in our cultures and societies. Furthermore, we cannot purport to value equality, unless at the same time we make effective efforts to have inclusive rather than exclusive groups in our societies.

Cultures are significant influences in these decision-making processes. Cultures are not only sources of our value choices, but they make the wider dissemination of ideas and strategies for inclusiveness possible. Furthermore, we are more likely to accept the social value of inclusiveness when a critical mass of our populations makes inclusiveness a cultural priority in organizing our societies. We increase our social intelligence when we create cultural and social conditions that emphasize the importance of inclusiveness, as well as expand the common good and social justice.

The social value of inclusiveness is one of five social values that express social justice—equality, inclusiveness, diversity, cooperation, and openness. Just as concerns about equality underlie issues of inclusiveness, inclusiveness builds foundations for diversity, cooperation, and openness. We need many more people to express these social and cultural values in our societies today, or to use primarily one of these values in the context of other social justice values, in order to improve our present and future societies. Our collective efforts to achieve life-enhancing cultures are also more likely to occur when we apply these constructive values to our families, beliefs, social classes, cultures, and societies.

Diversity
Diversity is a third significant cultural value and cultural value choice that honors social differences, and often depends on assumptions about equality and inclusiveness. Like equality and inclusiveness, diversity is a worthwhile socially intelligent value and value choice that improves life outcomes for all members of populations, and has constructive consequences for social justice in societies and globalization.

Diversity may be thought of as a single goal, or a single constructive value, which accepts and embraces cultural varieties of people as essential for societies' well-being. Diversity is also practiced as one of a cluster of related constructive values and value choices which motivate individual and social behavior to accept and celebrate social differences.

When we achieve more equality and inclusiveness in our cultures and societies—with increased public support for these values, value choices, and priorities—we establish social conditions that embrace complex rich cultural differences in our populations. Even though power may not be readily thought of as being achieved by diversity, social intelligence confirms that diverse populations are more powerful, better coordinated, and more resilient, than those that are ridden with prejudice, discrimination, and conflicts. From the broad perspectives of social intelligence diverse societies are more effective in formulating and achieving a common good and social justice, than societies that resist or ignore diversity as a viable cultural ideal, goal, or way of life.

History shows us that some societies were geographically closer to people of different races, ethnicities, cultures, and religions than others. Although tensions between different groups may not have been resolved in these situations, wherever it was possible to coexist peacefully without oppression, the cultural value of diversity was established. However, to the extent that cultural and social tensions among different groups were kept in check by the authoritarian powers of individuals or groups, destructive social conditions of oppression, exploitation, social castes, and slavery made diversity impossible.

History reveals that because many societies grew and developed in isolation from one another, their populations remained essentially unchallenged by groups different from themselves. Many homogeneous societies did not have to deal with challenges of diversity until more recent times, for example, so they often developed complex internal ways to establish status or power differences within themselves, such as castes or social classes.

However, our modern cultural ideal of diversity is based on more than these historical origins of the beginnings of peaceful coexistence. For example, today we associate the cultural ideal of diversity with having high or more just cultural and moral standards, perhaps because a significant aspect of diversity is to establish social conditions for peaceful coexistence. For example, we nurture positive public acceptance of cultural and social diversity in modern societies through shared assumptions that cultural differences make us more adept at dealing with globalization. In more advanced civilizations, and according to the principles of social intelligence, whenever compatibility among different races, ethnic groups, genders, and sexual orientations increases, we gain tangible benefits and increase our well-being.

IX. Social Justice

Often such public acceptance of the cultural ideal of diversity is hard won. However, even though there may still be some tumultuous, bloody conflicts between rival groups in our societies, or between societies, the most significant social fact is that we can learn to coexist peacefully with others. For example, we have already learned to appreciate—and value—some of the social and cultural differences among societies, and among groups within societies. Although diversity is necessarily a cultural ideal—a goal which cannot be fully realized—we know that we are headed in constructive directions when we make commitments to work toward achieving this cultural ideal and goal.

Social intelligence encourages us to embrace diversity in our quests for social justice. From the pragmatic viewpoints of social intelligence, establishing diversity in our cultures and societies not only expresses our values of equality and inclusiveness, but enlivens social and cultural conditions in modern societies. For example, we cannot meet the challenges of secularization and globalization adequately, unless we accept diversity. Accepting diversity is a critical stage of working out broad social issues about globalization in our worlds of today and tomorrow.

Socially intelligent ways of doing things help to advance social strategies to achieve diversity. For example, we learn about diversity more deeply when we trace diversity in our families, beliefs, social classes, cultures, and societies. We not only discover social facts related to patterns of behavior that resist or support diversity, but we also see deep-seated aspects of our shared resistance to diversity, especially when we are fearful of people and groups we do not know.

Even though our visceral reactions or resistance to diversity may express physiological aspects of our existential challenges to survive, social intelligence helps us to see how our emotional reactions can be at least temporarily overcome by considering our situations from broad cultural and social perspectives. Increasing social intelligence and achieving social justice enable us to enrich our individual and collective lives by embracing diversity.

Cooperation

Cooperation is a fourth significant cultural value and cultural value choice that is often associated with equality and social justice in modern societies. Like equality, inclusiveness, and diversity, cooperation is an example of a worthwhile socially intelligent value and value choice, which has constructive social consequences for societies and globalization.

Cooperation can be thought of as a single goal, or a single constructive value, which motivates and orients individual and social behavior toward taking collective action. Cooperation can also be thought of as one of a cluster of related constructive values and value choices which support working together to achieve socially intelligent goals.

One of the associations of cooperation with social justice in modern societies is that we need to work collectively in order to achieve the goals of social justice. For example, we must cooperate largely for pragmatic reasons, because we are more effective when we work together toward our shared goals, than when we work in isolation from each other. Isolated actions are necessarily less well-coordinated, as well as more fragmented, than collective efforts. We also gain benefits from diverse inputs to our work whenever we cooperate with others. Thus, encouraging cooperation among strong, independent historical actors is our most effective way to achieve socially intelligent goals for social justice.

Although during times of family, community, national, and international crisis we often band together to act cooperatively, our shared tendencies to cooperate with each other are usually less dominant than our inclinations to compete or enter into conflicts with each other. Furthermore, even when groups decide to cooperate with each other in order to achieve agreed-on goals, the give-and-take of cooperation is easily sabotaged or destroyed when one or a few individuals decide not to cooperate with the rest.

Because of this intrinsic fragility of cooperation, and because of the self-centeredness of many individuals and groups, cooperation is a cultural ideal rather than a social reality. For example, even in families where cooperation helps relatives to survive, once immediate needs are met cooperation may cease. In the long run, however, to the extent that families continue to meet their most vulnerable members' special needs, cooperation persists.

Other social groups and communities are often larger and less interdependent than families, with the result that they are less able to cooperate effectively for long periods of time. Nevertheless, when groups succeed in working together cooperatively, they often accomplish their goals and endure. Social intelligence suggests that cooperation is beneficial and encourages meaningful exchanges in groups or communities, even though cooperation is still largely a cultural ideal rather than a social reality.

We increase our interests and actions when we cooperate with others. When we aspire to this cultural ideal we are motivated and oriented to be more aware of opportunities to cooperate. This cultural awareness also makes us recognize when we already cooperate with others, even though we may not have previously realized that we were cooperating. Consequently, when we expect ourselves to cooperate now, we are more likely to cooperate.

In large part, we learn how to cooperate by following others' examples, or by deliberately making commitments to increase cooperation in our everyday lives. When we need to accomplish particular tasks at work, for example, we may choose to experiment by cooperating rather than competing with our colleagues. Thus looking for opportunities to cooperate with others teaches us how to cooperate to accomplish immediate tasks, long term attitudes, and social justice goals.

Social intelligence suggests that our most effective collective actions are cooperative. Because we are interdependent human beings, we need to find constructive ways to deal with our interdependence through being cooperative rather than competitive. Furthermore, increasing our emphases on cooperation rather than competition eventually decreases the power of competition in our societies, which neutralizes some of the destructive consequences of social classes in our cultures and societies.

Being cooperative with others is often as significant as being equal, and both equality and cooperation describe power relations with each other. For example, we act as though each person has equal power, in order to work together to meet shared goals cooperatively. Similarly, just as it takes effort to maintain our equality with others, we need to work at strengthening our inclinations to be cooperative.

Social intelligence encourages us to look for cooperation in our families, beliefs, social classes, cultures, and societies. However, it is through deliberately choosing cooperation as a cultural ideal and value, that we gradually accomplish most changes in these social influences, cultures, and societies. Paying attention to cooperation—both as a cultural ideal and the most effective way to work with others—destabilizes and resolves some of the most entrenched and intractable cultural and social problems in our societies, as well as advances social justice.

Openness

Openness is the fifth significant cultural value and cultural value choice to be considered together with equality, inclusiveness, diversity, and cooperation. Like equality, inclusiveness, diversity, and cooperation, openness is an example of a worthwhile socially intelligent value and value choice that has constructive social consequences for social justice in societies and globalization.

Openness can be thought of as a single goal, or as a single constructive value, which motivates and orients individual and social behavior to think and act expressly to improve communications and societies. Openness is also one of a cluster of related constructive values and value choices that enhance our capacities to learn how to change our cultures and societies.

For example, openness is a precondition for achieving effective equality. We need to put our cards on the table by conducting open communications, in order to establish level playing fields between two or more individuals, families, groups, communities, and societies. We are not equal players in complex social situations, for example, unless we are forthcoming about information and suggestions for decisions and commitments that increase individual and social well-being. We may have equal rights, but we also have responsibilities to consider others as equals in our actions, which need to be discussed openly.

Inclusiveness is another integral, necessary component in the quality of our open communications with others. We orient our actions toward expressing particular values, in order to size up complex social situations satisfactorily. For example, being selective in our value choices helps us to be objective, and enables us to be more direct and honest in describing and explaining where we are coming from, as we increase inclusiveness in our societies and globalization. We articulate our universalistic, holistic approaches in problem-solving, so that the tasks necessary for solving particular problems through openness are completed more effectively.

Diversity is also strengthened through openness. Because we may find it difficult to truly welcome different others into our families, communities, societies, or globalization, this may be a particularly challenging value to implement in our daily lives and communities. We need to go beyond merely giving lip service to diversity, for example, so that applying openness in our strategies—as well as in our uses of social intelligence principles—becomes a significant catalyst for accomplishing our goals. We must also realize that openness is essential to improving the quality and effectiveness of our social exchanges, including those in our families and personal intimacies, so that we continue to be direct in communicating whatever it is we want to accomplish and what our preferences are.

In these ways openness makes cooperation real rather than phony. We must level with others—through articulating our innermost thoughts and desires—before we can proceed to work with them to increase the common good or social justice. The quality of our cooperation depends on openness, as well as the results of our collective efforts and well-being. When we perpetuate openness, and establish this as a habit which honors others as well as ourselves, we are more socially intelligent, effective historical actors, and more satisfied with our everyday lives.

Openness is particularly important to establish in our families, which are foundations of our social intelligence. Even when we communicate with infants, toddlers, or ill family members, we need to use openness in our exchanges as much as possible. For example, being open and honest opens up relationships which are often overburdened with emotional stresses, so that whole families benefit from our clear intentions and goals. Being open and honest with our most significant others—spouses, siblings, adult children, young children, or family elders—is a critical principle of social intelligence, which increases our capacities to make cultural and social changes.

Sometimes using the five cultural values of equality, inclusiveness, diversity, cooperation, and openness is too difficult, even though we are highly motivated to accomplish social justice. However, social intelligence suggests that most of us need to examine whatever we want to accomplish in each of the five major social spheres of families, beliefs, social classes, cultures, and societies. Consequently, patterns in the cultural values of equality, inclusiveness, diversity, cooperation, and openness can also be examined through our families, beliefs, social classes, cultures, and societies. This social intelligence principle ensures that our actions are guided by social intelligence and social justice.

We need not strive to be rigorously objective or meticulously attentive with regard to finding constructive cultural values in our families, values, social classes, cultures, and societies. Rather, we need to assess and reassess our situations, so that we can focus more directly on our work of unlearning our biases, prejudices, and discriminatory practices. For example, when we deliberately clear contradictory concerns from our individual and social perspectives, we are better prepared to pursue our preferred social justice objectives with enthusiasm and determination.

Changing Cultures

X. Responsibilities as Historical Actors

When we are sufficiently socially intelligent, we see that we—and others—are inevitably historical actors. This means that whatever we decide to do, whether we act according to some plan or not, affects ourselves, others, and the universe. Even though we may passively follow lines of least resistance in our ways of being and doing in the world, or actively resist doing anything, we are all historical actors at all times.

Furthermore, there is no escape from the social fact of the inevitability of our being historical actors, whether we want this to be so or not, and whether we believe this or not. Our being alive counts, so the existential conditions of our situations must be considered and acknowledged if we are to live fully, especially as responsible historical actors.

Social intelligence helps us to come to terms with the social fact of being historical actors. Social intelligence also enables us to be more aware historical actors, so that we make wise value choices to guide our lives. For example, social intelligence shows us how to establish meaningful priorities, so that we align ourselves with our deepest values more clearly in going about our daily activities.

Social intelligence draws our attention to the significance of cultures in our world views as well as our orientations to others and ourselves. When we concern ourselves with social or cultural changes, for example, we need to examine past, present, and future cultures, in order to discover their dominant patterns, and know what it is that we really want to change. Although our cultures do not determine our fates, they are strong influences on whether or not we succumb to contemporary trends and pressures in our societies.

Cultures and Social Intelligence

We need to remember that cultures are significant determinants of cultural and social changes whenever we set about meeting our responsibilities as historical actors. However, in order to deal with complex nuances in our present and futures, and in order to live up to our responsibilities as historical actors, we must understand cultures sufficiently through time, as well as how cultures have impacted our individual lives and societies. We need to question, for example, how cultures define our different civilizations, as well as what cultures we prefer and choose for our future societies.

Social intelligence makes us aware of cultural influences that affect our decisions and commitments. This is especially important because unless we aim to make wise decisions, we cannot be sure that our actions express our deepest values. Similarly, unless we enter into thoughtful commitments, our actions may not reflect our long term interests in particular priorities and value choices.

Making decisions and commitments challenges us to ask—and answer—important basic questions about our responsibilities as historical actors. For example, we choose to deal with issues that deepen our understanding about our cultures and ourselves. Our questions tap into the power and complexities of cultural influences, so that we increase our knowledge about our particular social conditions. How do we decide which values to incorporate in our everyday activities, as well as which commitments to make? How does social intelligence guide us, so that we express our cultural preferences, resist being diverted, and pursue wise value choices with strong motivations to succeed?

We look to our cultures for inspiration in our socially intelligent actions to achieve cultural and social changes. Social intelligence helps us to better understand why we find particular values and beliefs meaningful, for example, so that we create ways to increase our senses of purpose through our value choices. Thus, social intelligence and cultural perspectives help us to get more established in our journeys toward fulfillment, because the improvements we accomplish are shared by all. Furthermore, when we aim to increase the common good and social justice, we are more likely to gain satisfaction from our socially intelligent actions to enrich our cultures.

Whenever we have doubts about our vocations, missions, and purposes, we are refreshed by returning to the principles of social intelligence. For example, social intelligence perspectives help us to size up the shifting sands of cultural and social changes. This is useful because participating in change processes is often deeply disconcerting, partly because everything we thought was real in our cultures and societies needs to be questioned. However, these difficult and challenging preliminary stages of accomplishing cultural and social changes are predictable, and we merely need to weather them by holding on to social intelligence principles. We can be assured that social intelligence sustains our efforts to increase the common good and social justice in the long run.

Remembering Cultures

We become responsible historical actors by increasing our social intelligence and acting according to principles of social intelligence. Social intelligence guides us to identify, understand, and take action in relation to significant broad social influences in our daily lives. For example, we need to remember to maintain our awareness about the major social influences of families, beliefs, social classes, cultures, and societies in how we make decisions, commitments, and predictions about our future worlds. Furthermore, as we use social intelligence principles to continue to learn about the power and complexities of our cultures, we realize crucial ways in which our decisions, commitments, and predictions are influenced by our cultures.

Our cultures provide us with the essence of our capacities to make moral and ethical decisions, as well as of our capacities to formulate and express value choices. For example, symbolic aspects of our past, present, and future cultures give us meanings and knowledge about how to conduct ourselves, what we want to do with our lives, and how we want to accomplish our goals. All in all, we are human because of our cultures and beliefs, and we base our actions on the mass of cultural impressions in which we are immersed at all times.

Social intelligence helps us to prioritize our lives, so that we deepen those meanings that we care about the most. For example, we become more whole when we increase our social intelligence, because social intelligence requires us to discard contradictory or incompatible cultural beliefs and values that do not help us to achieve our socially intelligent goals. We also benefit from focusing on making cultural and social changes to expand the common good and social justice, because this purposeful direction increases our own and others' fulfillment.

One of our most socially intelligent meaningful priorities is to consider the determining influences of cultures in our everyday lives, and in our plans for the present and future. We unsnarl our personal troubles, social issues, and social problems by examining the broad social and cultural influences that affect us, for example, and through understanding that we usually have more direct access to changing our cultures than changing our societies.

Our cultural experiences give us direct contacts with cultural values and social influences. For example, some of the cultural patterns we participate in—such as education—have meanings that impact our social statuses as well as our knowledge. Consequently, social intelligence cautions us to recognize that cultural processes are often much more than they seem.

We cannot afford to give up hopes of having strong and direct impacts on the substance of our cultures. Even though politicians or business leaders frequently manipulate cultures negatively, by supporting those who have the most economic means, we are all participants in cultural processes that define current and future social realities and priorities.

Social intelligence helps us to remember that cultures are important dimensions of social change, and that we have the greatest effects on our cultures when we choose to work collectively with others. For example, we may accomplish this by participating in social movements that increase public support for less popular values, such as peace in times of war. Or by entering into local community exchanges, so that we make rents more affordable for members of lower social classes. In each case we address values and priorities that impact current cultural patterns. Consequently, we often have constructive impacts on social changes by establishing new cultural priorities collectively.

We become responsible historical actors through focusing on patterns in our past and present cultures. For example, we assess particular aspects of our cultures when we collect social facts about our communities' educational resources. We also research and develop our communities' shared educational purposes, in order to galvanize sufficient political will to increase social justice by meeting communities' educational needs. Furthermore, we use social intelligence principles to design strategies to ease cultural pressures that limit the effectiveness of communities' educational facilities.

Our most balanced social interventions use social intelligence principles to focus on our cultures and our access to cultural resources. Social intelligence helps us to remember the importance of cultures in social changes, and guides us to act consistently in relation to complex and powerful ongoing cultural influences. When we consider our cultural options first, we clarify our visions of realistic cultural and social changes for improved futures.

Cultures Through Time

Responsible historical actors balance time perspectives in whatever they decide to do to bring about cultural and social changes. For example, social intelligence shows us how to inform our plans with knowledge about past patterns of cultural and social influences; how to use present social facts to understand and manage the most compelling cultural and social influences in our current situations; and how to design visions of better futures as precisely as possible.

One of the most significant social facts about cultures is that past and continuing traditions play powerful roles in determining current individual and social decisions. When we consider our pasts from the points of view of evolution rather than history, we see that before histories were recorded, traditional solutions to social issues served as rich but limited resources. Although the beginnings of civilizations as well as their foundations derive from traditions, traditions remain relatively stable or static for long periods of time, and therefore often restrict the flexibility necessary to adapt to changing circumstances.

However, in order to understand the past through the broad cultural and social perspectives of social intelligence, we often remember cultures by honoring the power and complexities of traditions. Understanding traditions of the past helps us to come to terms with the present and the future, for example, especially because many traditions persist to today, even though their functions and rationales may have changed. Consequently, it is unwise for members of modern societies to undervalue traditions, or underestimate their power and complexities.

Social intelligence shows us that traditions may still be considered as foundations of our current societies and civilizations, even though fewer people base their lives on the day-to-day dictates of traditions. Therefore, traditions are powerful starting points in understanding our cultural and social origins when we see the hold that traditions had—and may still have—over matters of life and death, especially in relation to human survival.

The most easily recognized carriers of social traditions in our cultures are religions. Even though politics and education are also strongly influenced by traditional approaches to understanding the world, many political and educational views derive from religious sources. Social facts and social intelligence show us that people survived by following customs and traditions before religions developed. For example, religions were often organized through community customs, and religious leaders were family and community elders. Later, religious denominations were developed by charismatic leaders who based their work on traditions from the cultural, social, and historical circumstances in which members of their religious groups lived.

In considering cultures through time, and how we arrived at the cultures we have today, we need to appreciate the endurance of cultural traditions, in spite of their limitations in solving current social problems or social change issues. However, when we are socially intelligent we see that traditional practices may have useful rituals—secular rituals, as well as religious or political rituals—that help us to build communities in times of rapid social change and alienation. Thus, traditions are a social reality that we cannot afford to ignore, whose power and complexities we recognize in order to manage our cultural and social situations effectively.

Responsible historical actors acknowledge the cultural and social significance of traditions in designing viable cultural and social changes. We understand the power and complexities of traditions in our own lives—in our families and beliefs as well as in social classes and the times in which we live. Our cultural conflicts also need to be considered in terms of traditions, if we are to act with others to design alternatives to traditions that are particularly harsh, rigid, or restrictive. Thus, even though some cultural traditions persist to the present day in our most modern societies, responsible historical actors need to question their effectiveness in meeting and satisfying ongoing contemporary needs.

Broad socially intelligent views of individuals and societies, which include evolutionary perspectives, help us to see some of the creature comforts that unproductive traditions and rituals bring to today's societies. Although traditions are often relatively harmless additions to the richness of our contemporary cultures, responsible historical actors must continue to ask whether some traditions still serve the common good and social justice.

Other aspects of cultures through time are traditions of cultural and social ways to make ongoing collective decisions and commitments, especially in relation to accepted standards of right and wrong. When we are responsible historical actors, we may choose to establish informed standards of ethical appropriateness, for example, as we design ways to honor cultures of the past and present in creating better cultures for the future.

Decisions

Decisions are pivotal points of our participation in our cultures. Decisions are important because they usually move us into action, and even though social intelligence helps us to think about social influences differently, it is our actions that make real differences in our worlds.

Decisions and their follow-up actions also move us toward making commitments, which is how we make transitions from increasing our social intelligence in trial and error ways, to make deep resolves to pursue particular purposes and directions in our lives. We make these more substantial decisions based on those cultural meanings that affect us the most.

Thus our cultures and meanings are significant motivators in how we make both our decisions and our commitments, especially in how we define our responsibilities as historical actors. When we focus on our decision-making, for example, we see that we often find it easier to act when meanings are associated with our actions. These meanings include symbols of the values we attribute to our actions, but they must also be sufficient to motivate us to formulate specific goals in relation to our situations.

Until we become interested in social intelligence, and willing to apply social intelligence principles to different aspects of our everyday lives, we may not give much serious thought to how we make our decisions about those cultural values we choose to direct our actions. Our decisions are vital links in the chains of actions that culminate in reaching our goals effectively. Although we may remember to design strategies in order to proceed with our projects, we may neglect to make decisions about which goals to aim for to increase our life satisfaction and make real differences in our families, communities, and societies.

Cultures persist wherever we are, and whatever we are doing. For example, just as religions have rules to live by to achieve the holy life, we can also choose secular values to guide us to increase the common good and social justice. Cultivating secular goals does not eliminate possibilities that our religions may lead us in meaningful directions for spiritual fulfillment, but rather suggests that we should use both religious and secular cultural values in our everyday decisions. Just as religion is more than a one-day-a-week proposition, being guided by social intelligence is an everyday, everywhere deal.

The more we move from living hand-to-mouth—by reacting to social conditions as they occur—to developing our awareness about how many decisions we make each day and how we make them, the more we prepare ourselves for making meaningful effective decisions. Wanting to neutralize what appeared to be random conditions in our lives helps us to be receptive to social intelligence principles, so that we start to make decisions differently. Furthermore, when we make these decisions, we benefit from cultures as inspirations for our actions.

Cultures inform our decisions in many ways, and being socially intelligent means that we are selective in choosing values to enlighten and enhance our decisions. We change from having very little awareness of the value associations and implications of our decisions, for example, to being cautious about which cultural values we want to express and honor through our actions. We may decide that particular religious or secular values should guide us, for example, and social intelligence helps us to make these value choices come alive. We are increasingly able to use our knowledge of social facts to make decisions and act in a variety of social situations.

In the beginning of our efforts to understand social intelligence and increase our social intelligence, our decisions do not necessarily appear to be influenced by cultural issues and concerns. However, in reflecting about and assessing the usefulness of our recent decisions—which we made in the spirit of applying social intelligence principles—we can determine whether these new decisions improve our own and others' lives. Furthermore, scrutinizing how we make our decisions, as well as the outcomes of our decisions, provides us with sufficient social facts to assess whether we should continue to make decisions and commitments based on particular values.

Our decisions necessarily reflect our most significant value choices, and social intelligence helps us to distinguish between value choices which are constructive or destructive, self-oriented or collectivity-oriented, and life-enhancing or death-directed. Also, we try—individually and collectively—to cultivate socially intelligent values such as equality, inclusiveness, diversity, cooperation, and openness. Thus, becoming more aware of the cultural and social contexts of our decision-making helps us to recognize how cultures influence our decisions and their cultural or social consequences.

Commitments

Our commitments refer to our being responsible historical actors even more directly than our decisions, because our commitments are lived as clusters of related decisions that move us in consistent directions, perhaps for a lifetime. Social intelligence suggests that we need to examine our commitments, to ensure that they move us forward to achieve cultural meanings, purposes, and directions that ring true. This scrutiny is necessary because we are often asked to make commitments when we are too young or immature to recognize what their social or cultural consequences and implications are.

Our commitments are made at deeper levels than our everyday decisions, but they ultimately derive from our most significant decisions. When our commitments endure, they are difficult to change, even though social intelligence principles may suggest ways to adapt or reshape our commitments when needed. However, before we make new commitments, it is socially intelligent to examine our existing commitments in light of our ongoing cultural value choices.

As we apply social intelligence principles to our daily decisions, we see meaningful differences between living our lives with or without social intelligence. This may inspire us to make commitments to increase our social intelligence, to be responsible historical actors, and to work with others toward increasing social justice. For example, social intelligence helps us to see more cultural connections in our lives, so that we understand the many challenges involved in making particular value choices. We may explore contemporary meanings of constructive, collectivity-oriented, life-enhancing cultural values—such as equality, inclusiveness, diversity, cooperation, and openness—in our everyday lives.

We may also look more closely at the five major social influences that social intelligence focuses on, in order to understand their power and complexities, and in order to assess social and cultural contexts in making new commitments. This means that we try to identify social needs that can be met through our commitments to our families, beliefs, social classes, cultures, or societies.

One important characteristic we notice about our families, as we consider making new value choices in our commitments, is that many of our families' interactions past and present are emotion-laden, rather than thoughtful and considered. This holds true for all families, whatever their social or cultural circumstances, in that families are essentially emotional systems of reactive interactions—at least latently if not overtly. We may decide, however, that we want to make commitments to write or diagram our families' histories, to show how family members repeat particular patterns of interaction in different generations. This helps family members to be more objective about their social, cultural, and emotional origins.

In addition we need to scrutinize our beliefs closely, in order to assess how our religious or secular values influence our decisions and commitments, and how our cultures influence our strongest beliefs. This enables us to cultivate those cultural beliefs that mean the most to us. For example, we try to eliminate contradictions in our cultural beliefs, which inevitably dilute our efforts or prevent us from being effective in our decisions and commitments. Because social intelligence emphasizes the crucial influences that beliefs have on our behavior, we make sure that our commitments express our most meaningful beliefs, as well as beliefs that reflect our deepest understanding of cultures and social changes.

Becoming more aware of social class cultures, and how these impact our lives, is useful for assessing the value choices we make in our cultures and commitments. Most of us take our social class cultures and commitments for granted, so that we may tend to believe that social class differences are "right" or "natural." Because of this social fact, social intelligence helps us to counteract these tendencies by encouraging us to be objective and critical of social classes, in order to make wiser commitments. For example, we take the multiple social class cultures of modern societies into consideration—such as social classes based on education, race, ethnicity, gender, sexual orientation, age, and ablebodiedness—as well as the more traditional social class bases of social connections and material assets, when we make new commitments.

Examining our cultural habits in the context of our cultures shows us how we accept particular cultures—such as social class cultures or religious traditions—more than others. We need to understand where we are coming from, with respect to our cultural likes and dislikes, for example, before we can be sufficiently knowledgeable to commit ourselves to particular cultural values. Furthermore, social intelligence helps to connect the cultural components of our everyday decisions to what we want to achieve through commitments to cultural goals. This prepares us to be responsible historical actors, by cooperating with others to achieve broad cultural and social changes.

Lastly, considering our cultural commitments in the broadest perspectives of our societies highlights the importance of history in determining how we understand our responsibilities as historical actors. Because the present is always history in the making, our historical views of our cultures and cultural commitments are important. However, what we choose to honor through our value choices varies, depending on our cultural preferences and experiences.

For example, if we have been prejudiced or discriminated against because of our genders or sexual orientations, we may be more committed to pursuing social justice in these areas, than to solving social problems related to economic or material social class differences. Therefore, we use broad societal views of social injustices related to genders and sexual orientations to deepen our capacities to make meaningful commitments, by linking our commitments to preferred value choices.

Meaning and Change

Meaning is a component of our cultures, and our cultures are effective ways to bring about a wide variety of social changes. Meanings make us human, and civilizations prioritize and define meanings, as well as depend on them for their societies' survival and fulfillment. With regard to our personal meanings, social intelligence helps us to appreciate the extent to which we are motivated by meanings, so that life itself can be thought of as quests for meaning.

Because meaning is a central aspect of our everyday lives, it becomes an effective vehicle of cultural and social change. Also, because meaning is one of the most significant results or functions of our cultures, important cultural and social changes flow from introducing new meanings into our cultures and societies. Sometimes this is achieved through technological inventions, for example, or through shifts in political or economic alliances with other countries. Globalization has significant influences on less dominant cultures in the international community, but at the same time the most dominant cultures have to remain open to the impacts of contrasting cultures if they are to be enriched and move with the times.

Meanings shift in our cultures, depending on the frames of reference that are used to establish meanings that resonate with populations. However, our most central meanings cannot be too far outside established domains of knowledge, for example, because they will not be understood by sufficient people. Relatively unknown aspects of social changes—as reported in serious newspapers—are critical topics for us to research by gathering significant cultural and social facts. These facts keep our decisions and commitments well-informed and well-prepared for whatever actions we need to take.

We change our life courses when we are educated, and when we make commitments to pursue higher education or further education. The additional attention we give to cultural and social facts in our education makes us less likely to accept the status quo of the cultural and social conditions of our personal lives. We are also less likely to be passive about cultural and social changes that are beneficial in our societies, so that they gradually improve the quality of life for all members of our populations.

Because individual and social apathy are problematic in contemporary societies, we need to consider how to transform cultural meanings into motivations and political will. For example, we educate people to help them to increase meanings in their lives and make commitments to better their situations or increase their life satisfaction.

One of our choices in increasing meaning, especially in how we conduct ourselves daily, is to learn about social intelligence, and to apply social intelligence to making decisions and commitments about who we are and what we want to accomplish. Although this search for new meanings is by no means synonymous with education, social intelligence includes increasing our knowledge of social facts, so that we make more informed and more enlightened decisions and commitments. Social intelligence also makes us more objective about the many options we have in our cultural choices and value choices about interpreting social facts and meanings.

When we decide to be responsible historical actors, we understand that controlling meanings is an important aspect of our motivations and accomplishments, especially when we work with others. We are more responsible in our actions, for example, when we use meanings deliberately in our personal decisions and commitments, as well as in our work with others toward increasing the common good and social justice. We—and those with whom we work—need to be motivated by meanings that carry us forward, for example, as well as by meanings that continue to motivate us in harsh and difficult circumstances. Meanings are not superficial additions to improving the quality of our lives, but rather the life-blood of our most important endeavors and our strongest feelings.

The meanings we choose for our decisions and commitments guide us to find like-minded people who share our cultural values and value choices. For example, we work with others more compatibly and more effectively when we cherish similar deep-seated meanings. One of the primary benefits of becoming more socially intelligent is that we increase meaning in our lives, and become more active in searching for solutions to cultural and social issues that concern us. Meanings give us purposes for interacting with others and make our lives more fulfilling.

As we increase meanings in our actions, our senses of purpose in achieving goals as historical actors also increase. We are more responsible in our impacts on cultures when we stay close to the principles of social intelligence, as well as identify with our most significant meanings and purposes. In fact, we cannot consider what our responsibilities are—as historical actors—unless we explore issues of meaning and purpose in our behavior. We may need to redo some of our decisions and commitments when we come up with answers about what our primary meanings and purposes are, but this is one of the most important ways in which we maintain and increase our social intelligence.

Fulfillment and Change

Historical actors assume responsibilities for pursuing goals that lead to individual and social fulfillment, as well as goals that increase the common good and social justice. In fact, the cultural ideal of individual and social fulfillment may be what drives most of us to increase the common good and social justice. For example, we gain peace of mind from knowing that we are doing everything possible to resolve issues around the common good and social justice. Consequently, we are fulfilled by achieving both our personal goals and the common good or social justice.

Social intelligence teaches us that we accomplish complex cultural and social changes through our cultures. We do not have to wait for economic or political policy resolutions of social issues, but rather trust that small and large scale changes in cultures—perhaps with regard to education or political awareness—have strong, durable impacts on populations or civilizations. When we are responsible historical actors, we choose cultural goals that improve cultural and social conditions, because these strategies bring about constructive changes. For example, advertising companies and large corporations show us the power of cultures in social changes when they invest large sums of money to use cultural images and symbols for changing how we think about particular products and ourselves.

Having established the importance of cultural strategies to change cultures and societies, it is easier to be goal directed in becoming more socially intelligent, or in being responsible historical actors. Furthermore, when we understand the power and complexities of the five major social influences of families, beliefs, social classes, cultures, and societies, we consider making cultural changes that increase fulfillment in these significant spheres of interaction.

For example, we examine families in order to understand one of the most significant major social influences in our lives. Social intelligence helps us to see that having freedom in our families is a prerequisite for being fulfilled, and for enabling other family members to be fulfilled. In reality, however, our cultures and families often block our capacities to be free, because we are pressured to conform to relatives' cultural standards. Nevertheless, when we establish our independence in our families by making deliberate value choices, we at the same time create opportunities for relatives to increase their freedom and independence.

Similarly, when we consider our beliefs as another of the five major social influences in our lives, social intelligence guides us to establish a few of our deepest beliefs as means to accomplish cultural and social changes. If we decide to pursue truth through collecting cultural and social facts, for example, we are more likely to make effective cultural and social changes. Applying social intelligence principles deepens cultural beliefs in our identities, so that we make more authentic value choices in our actions. We collect cultural and social facts to substitute more meaningful beliefs for contradictory or less effective beliefs, in order to strengthen our cultural purposes to bring about significant social changes.

The major social influence of social classes includes cultural forces, and values that uphold social classes may be challenged or replaced by alternative value choices. Value considerations are important, because social intelligence emphasizes that social classes are traditional ways to organize societies which have significant impacts on the qualities of our lives. For example, when we prioritize the value of cooperation rather than competition in our exchanges with others, this new cultural choice initiates cultural and social changes that increase fulfillment in populations rather than social class strife.

Finding cultural means to increase fulfillment through our cultures includes considering education together with the value choice of equality. According to social intelligence principles knowledge depends partially on life experiences, so that all people's experiences need to be considered in building knowledge. This helps us to see new ways to develop and use knowledge. Furthermore, applying the principle of equality in our cultural mission to improve education helps us to be more socially intelligent and purposeful in making meaningful fulfillment possible for more people.

We also need to look at societies in considering the power and complexities of the five major social influences in our shared experiences. When we consider historical cultural changes, for example, we see that cultural taboos—such as homosexuality—harmed whole societies through ignorance, prejudice, and discrimination. Consequently, we use laws to protect the rights of all members of our populations today, so that we increase capacities for fulfillment. For example, we cannot benefit from having privileges such as widely accepted sexual identities, when others are not accorded the same rights. We need responsible historical actors to bring about laws which ensure all people rights, in order to increase fulfillment for all.

These examples show how fulfillment results from making specific cultural changes through families, beliefs, social classes, cultures, and societies. Because societies must adapt through time, populations pay attention to cultural initiatives undertaken by responsible historical actors. We come full circle in our missions to be responsible historical actors, when we make value choices that lead to the greater fulfillment of more people in our cultures and societies.

XI. Social Realities and Cultures

Although we usually consider that the primary significance of cultures is their meanings and symbols, cultures also inspire changes when we think of them in relation to the five major social influences of families, beliefs, social classes, cultures, and societies. For example, because religions are integral parts of cultures and civilizations, we can scrutinize social facts and social realities related to religious meanings and religious views of social changes. Social intelligence guides us in this endeavor with the result that fact-finding about social realities such as religions leads to innovative cultural and social changes.

Assessing social realities in our own situations is a starting point for becoming more aware of our capacities to be socially intelligent and apply principles of social intelligence to our everyday decisions and commitments. For example, we are active participants in cultural and social changes when we cultivate social intelligence and pursue goals that increase the common good and social justice. In fact, our effectiveness in making socially intelligent changes depends on our assessments of the social facts of our situations, as well as on our interpretations of the cultural and social meanings of those social facts that we care about the most.

One way to understand the significance of social realities in our cultures and social intelligence is to consider how we become more objective when we increase our social intelligence. We use the broad perspectives of social intelligence to create new knowledge from social facts, through examining the cultural and social influences of families, beliefs, social classes, cultures, and societies. This allows us to regulate our individual and collective effectiveness through analyzing and interpreting these social facts. Our increased objectivity shows us that social facts matter, and that social realities guide us to become more responsible for our actions. For example, we understand more fully whether meeting or not meeting particular goals increases the common good and social justice.

Because cultures are complex and powerful social influences, which guide us to initiate some of our most important innovative cultural and social changes, we examine cultures to find social realities that express our successes and failures in meeting our objectives. We also assess whether or not our actions are sufficiently responsible, depending on the social facts of their results, and the relationships of these social facts to our socially intelligent goals.

Such fact-finding enquiries guide this chapter of *Cultures and Social Intelligence*. For example, we focus on social realities or patterns of social facts in the five major social influences of our family cultures, cultural beliefs, social class cultures, cultures, and societies as well as social justice. This approach grounds our social intelligence in social facts, and makes our cultural innovations more realistic and more effective.

Our family cultures are foundations of our social intelligence—individually and collectively—which means that they are often difficult to change, or slow to change, even given the specific focus in *Cultures and Social Intelligence* of bringing about cultural changes in our families. For example, our families' social facts show us that patterns of behavior repeat from generation to generation, and that family members frequently dysfunction rather than relate to each other in new ways within their family cultures.

Social realities in our cultural beliefs are expressed through our religions, education, lifestyles, and consumer behavior as well as our families. For example, we often entertain and nurture cultural beliefs that were expressed by our family elders, or cultural beliefs that are the most meaningful for us. Testing our cultural beliefs with social realities is a socially intelligent strategy that opens our eyes to more practical options for making value choices, so that we accomplish what we really want to do.

The social realities of social class cultures, cultures, and societies give us frames of reference to understand our everyday communications, so that we recognize how often we may unwittingly reinforce restrictive or destructive social class differences. Whether we realize this or not, our lifestyles result largely from choosing cultural values that indirectly—but powerfully—reinforce status and social class differences. However, we can change some of these social realities when we make more socially intelligent value choices, especially those that decrease our unquestioned assumptions about traditional social class contrasts within and among our societies.

Social intelligence also guides us to choose the cultural value of social justice in relation to our cultural and social realities. The new knowledge and effective know-how of social intelligence helps us to make more enlightened changes in how we conduct our cultural and social business, so that improved futures become new cultural and social realities.

Social Realities of Family Cultures

When we consider that we are usually raised by our families to be moral beings, we realize that it is useful to trace our early understanding of right and wrong to the social facts of particular patterns in our families' interactions. Social intelligence encourages us to recognize that our families lay the foundations of our moral and emotional postures to ourselves, others, and the world. Social intelligence also helps us to be more objective about those social facts in our families that influence us the most, especially because patterns in our families' interactions are passed down from generation to generation.

Our families' cultures have distinctive values and value choices, depending on which values enable our families to survive, adapt, or achieve fulfillment through time. Sometimes our families' values are relatively traditional, or repeated many times through different generations. Our families' values may also be modern and new, perhaps having been developed during recent family crises or youthful family rebellions.

Some of these variations in families' cultures and values reflect families' emotional relationships. For example, closed family emotional systems are characterized by rigid cultural values and practices, which are not sufficiently flexible for the optimal growth and cultural development of their family members. By contrast, open family emotional systems often have wide ranges of flexible cultural values and practices, which support the growth and cultural development of their family members.

Another social reality that affects our families' cultures is the degree of cohesiveness of families. When families have relatively splintered structures—for example, through separations between their nuclear units and their extended kin groups—their cultures are more disjointed and less meaningful. However, separations between nuclear families and their extended kin can be bridged by individual family members, especially those who deliberately use their social intelligence to heal splintered relationships or factions in their families' cultures. When fragmented family cultures become more cohesive, their emotional systems protect their family members more effectively, and provide more socially intelligent guidance.

One of the negative consequences of fragmented family cultures is that nuclear families that are separated from their extended kin are easily overloaded by their emotional intensity, too much togetherness, and value choices that do not allow a healthy give and take among their family members. Characteristically, one member of isolated nuclear families tends to be dominant, so that the relative closure of these nuclear emotional systems leads to further fragmentations, such as conflicts or separations between nuclear family members.

Social intelligence helps us to deal with family pressures and emotional dependencies more objectively and more rationally, although emotional aspects of intense family exchanges inevitably resurface from time to time. Social intelligence recognizes the importance and emotional significance of our family cultures, largely because of the emotional content of our family communications. For example, families are different from other social groups because of their intense emotional interdependence rather than their similar blood links. In order to be socially intelligent we need to pay attention to our families' impacts, because of the considerable power that our families' emotions have over our lives.

Families' cultures are routinely passed to our children, but they also influence other family members at different points of our life cycles. Just as we are born into families who participate in certain cultural rituals and have cultural expectations about what birth means, we also die in families that practice particular rituals and have expectations about what death means. Thus, we cannot escape from the social facts and social realities of our families and their cultures, whether we want to or not. We are who we are in part due to the strong cultural and social influences of our upbringing, and ongoing adult family relationships.

Sometimes we feel compelled to geographically leave our families for a while, in order to be more objective about them, and to understand our socially intelligent options. For example, we frequently get so drawn into our families' togetherness that we stay stuck in some family relationships for years, decades, or a lifetime. In this situation our living, breathing family dependencies often cut us off from constructive social realities, rather than enhance our social intelligence and our capacities to increase the common good and social justice.

We change our families' cultures and our societies' cultures when we make different value choices in our family cultures. For example, we begin to question family traditions when we engage in new behavior, or help our families to adapt more effectively in crises—such as during the loss of a significant family member or a family migration. Socially intelligent interventions in our usual family interactions predictably open up closed family emotional systems, so that families' structures and ways of relating to each other become freer and more productive. These cultural innovations make considerable lasting differences to us, our families, family cultures, cultures, and societies.

Social Realities in Cultural Beliefs

Social realities are connected to cultural beliefs and to changing cultures, but they are not necessarily the substance or content of our cultural beliefs. We have beliefs about social realities—for example, our definitions of social reality are beliefs—but we also have beliefs about infinite aspects of our daily lives that are not social realities. In fact, there are often considerable gaps between our cultural beliefs and social realities, or between our cultural beliefs and the real circumstances of our social situations.

Gaps between our cultural beliefs and our social realities are particularly noticeable—often because we experience pain or hardship as a consequence—when our social ideals or expectations are not reinforced by the facts of our everyday lives. For example, when our beliefs are too far removed from social realities, we may decide to ignore or deny social realities rather than pay attention to them. However, we can also choose to change our cultural beliefs, so that there is a better fit between our cultural beliefs and the social realities that exist in our day-to-day lives.

Social intelligence requires that we look directly at—and assess—those social realities that affect our lives the most. For example, social intelligence encourages us to pursue cultural ideals as goals, so that we motivate ourselves and others to make constructive changes in restrictive social realities. These are productive purposes for temporarily ignoring social realities, and for temporarily denying the power of social realities. However, we should be extremely cautious about not facing up to the social facts of our particular situations in the long run, because when we do this we frequently miss opportunities to make necessary changes.

One of the ways to understand the abstract but powerful qualities of cultural beliefs is to review our cultural beliefs in relation to the social realities of our situations and societies. We get a clear picture of how we handle gaps between our cultural beliefs and social facts, for example, when we assess the extent to which we deal directly with social realities in our day-to-day decisions and commitments. When we apply social intelligence principles in our analyses, we not only begin to understand why gaps between our cultural beliefs and social realities exist, but we narrow these gaps by making cultural changes. For example, we choose new values and ideals to represent the facts of our social situations more accurately.

Issues related to changing our cultures are often clearer when we examine social realities in our cultural beliefs, than when we examine social realities in our families' cultures. This is so because our cultural beliefs relate to cultures outside our families' cultures as well as within them, so they give us broader bases of cultural information to direct our behavior and aspirations. Consequently, when we examine gaps between our cultural beliefs and social realities, these are not necessarily inward journeys, but rather explorations of how our cultural beliefs are connected to cultural and social realities, and how our beliefs can be changed through modifying these cultural and social connections.

When we use social intelligence to become more aware of our relationships to our cultures by examining our cultural beliefs and social realities, we gain more control over our value choices, as well as over our choices of cultural goals. Social intelligence perspectives show us that it is not so much the content of our cultural beliefs that determines our social realities, but how we use our cultural beliefs in relation to social realities and our exchanges with others.

Social intelligence suggests that our cultural beliefs must remain open if we are to make effective commitments to increase the common good and social justice. We cannot afford to separate our cultural beliefs from criticism, for example, or from assessing their impacts on social realities, because our beliefs need to serve us and others as reliable sources of motivation. When we use social intelligence principles we depend on our cultural beliefs to change our cultures, and we continue to assess their impacts on what we do and how others respond to our cultural changes. Thus we avoid the rigidity and bigotry of closed cultural beliefs, and work constructively toward inclusiveness and diversity.

When we change our cultures to forge better futures, we deliberately use cultures to open up new possibilities for meaningful social changes. Social intelligence guides us in this endeavor, as long as we continue to compare our cultural beliefs with the social realities that confront us when we work with others to accomplish cultural and social changes.

We use social facts to assess whether we are accomplishing our immediate goals of changing our cultures, and the extent of gaps or contradictions between our cultural goals and cultural change achievements. Even though social realities may not appear to be within our cultural beliefs, they surround them. Therefore, we must deal with social facts directly if we are to continue to be socially intelligent in our ongoing decisions, commitments, and actions.

Social Realities of Social Class Cultures

Social class cultures are recognizable and have a specificity that makes their presence relatively tangible. For example, we often identify social class cultures more easily than other dimensions of our cultures, and they frequently seem to be directly related to social realities. However, social classes also have strong social influences beyond the values and beliefs of our social class cultures, because they are firmly rooted in social realities such as material assets or levels of educational accomplishments. Thus social class realities are social forces to be reckoned with, both outside and within our social class cultures.

Social class cultures reflect the multiplicity of social class bases in modern societies—such as those defined by gender, sexual orientation, race, ethnicity, education, health, and ablebodiedness—as well as traditional social class differences according to social status connections and material assets. Social class cultures are made up of ideas, ideals, beliefs, expectations, and assumptions that we associate with different social classes, which reinforce the social class differences we live with in our day-to-day situations and societies. Even though we do not know whether social classes could persist without social class cultures, we see that social class cultures provide vital support for social classes.

Because there is overlap between social class cultures and social classes, social realities exist in both social classes and social class cultures. For example, social classes have power and impacts on our lives because their social realities go largely unchallenged, or unquestioned. We believe in social classes through our social class cultures, so that we often take social classes for granted in daily activities which are largely defined by our social classes. Thus social class realities are powerful but sometimes unrecognized influences in our lives, because of their hidden physical characteristics and their cultural underpinnings.

Aspiring to be socially mobile in modern societies is widely experienced as a side-effect of the power and complexities of social classes and their cultural beliefs. For example, big business and advertising impact our thinking about possibilities for social class mobility, so we consider it normal and natural to want to compete with others to be upwardly mobile. Even though we may realize that we choose social mobility as a cultural value, especially when we are socially intelligent, we also need to acknowledge the social fact that many people in our societies feel compelled to be socially mobile. However, this does not mean that we have to accept social class cultural values as our own, especially if we prefer to restrict or neutralize the power that social classes have in defining our shared social and material destinies.

Social intelligence helps us to counteract the impacts that social class cultures have on our lifestyles and value choices, by designing cultures that run counter to existing social classes in our societies. We may decide to think of education in its own right, for example, rather than merely as a vehicle of upward social mobility. Also, we may deliberately pursue careers that could change social class structures—such as public interest law—rather than perpetuate social class differences. Social intelligence shows us that social class cultures need to be questioned and changed rather than accepted, especially if we want to increase the common good and social justice.

At present, amidst the globalization of our market economies, social class cultures seem very real in our everyday decisions and commitments, as well as in ongoing social class structures. This social reality leads to social classes' dominance often going unchallenged. However, by contrast, social intelligence encourages us to carve out freedom in relation to social classes and social class cultures, so that we can eventually create social realities that do not reinforce social classes or social class cultures.

Our cultures inspire us to create socially intelligent options and alternatives to social classes. For example, we are free to make value choices that move us in constructive directions, such as increasing the common good and social justice. Socially intelligent choices include establishing more egalitarian social conditions, because we see that social classes and their cultures do not work well for large proportions of populations in different societies and civilizations.

Given the long history of social classes in cultures and societies, we see that social classes and their cultures have exacerbated social injustices rather than resolved them. Consequently, we need to both challenge and change the status quo of social class cultures and social class realities. In fact, changing social class realities and social class cultures may be essential for strengthening our cultures and civilizations for the future.

Social Realities in Cultures

Our cultures are the fourth of the five major social influences that form the substantive base of our social intelligence. Our cultures reflect existing social realities, and explain ongoing social realities, as well as describe future social realities. To the extent that our cultures provide us with accurate reflections, descriptions, and explanations of social realities, we can depend on our cultures for reliable information. However, our cultures may also distort social realities—for example, by presenting our own societies as superior to other societies— which confuses our cultural priorities and judgments about effective ways to accomplish vital tasks, such educating members of our youngest generations.

In addition to providing us with reliable information about our societies, our cultures give us important ways to change cultures and societies. For example, when we choose to be socially intelligent about how we see our worlds, social intelligence helps us to be more objective about our cultures. We prefer to make value choices that represent our deepest values, rather than have cultures that coerce us to conform to societies or to accommodate to others' expectations. We may also prefer to honor values that are not obvious or popular in modern societies—such as equality, inclusiveness, diversity, cooperation, and openness—which bring better futures into being.

Social intelligence does more than outline these constructive value choices in contemporary societies. The principles of social intelligence teach us that culture is one of our most effective means to bring about deep-seated cultural and social changes, especially those which affect our cultures and societies in the long run. For example, investing in better education for more members of our populations changes the quality of our cultures and our societies. However, in order to be sufficiently strong to have constructive impacts, our education systems must meet the needs of diverse populations, which include different genders, sexual orientations, races, ethnicities, and social classes.

Even with respect to our creature comforts and our basic postures to life, our cultures affect our social being, our imaginations, and our capacities to act constructively. Our orientations to ourselves, others, our communities, our societies, and the international community are strongly influenced by our cultures, even though our first perspectives derive from our families' cultures and we mature by interacting in varied cultures. For example, if our senses of humanity are not what we prefer, we can turn to our cultures to find alternative values that change our ways of thinking and doing.

Increasing contacts with cultures changes our attitudes and motivations. This is important because our chosen cultural meanings give us reasons to act, goals, and orientations to accomplish our goals. When we learn new languages, for example, we change our views and attitudes about societies, civilizations, and the world. Learning new languages enriches our education and our experiences, because learning different languages opens up and broadens our original societies' cultures. Social intelligence requires us to open our worlds and broaden our cultures in order to live fully and choose improved future worlds.

Social intelligence makes us aware of value choices that bring about personal, cultural, and social changes. Because the growth of munitions industries and increased political tensions threaten our existence in modern societies, we must deal with basic survival issues as well as assess the purposes of our lives. Although we need not be overly cautious about existential concerns, they are ever-present and need to be addressed as much as possible rather than ignored or denied.

Social intelligence responds to our needs for deep thinking by keeping us aware of the power and complexities of our cultural and social realities. Even though our families are particularly instrumental in forming the foundations of our social intelligence, we have continuous opportunities to change our social intelligence in different aspects of our lives if we so choose.

One of the most effective means of changing our social intelligence is to broaden our horizons by embracing new cultures, so that we become more objective and less ethnocentric about our original cultures. Although we inevitably remain biased to some extent by our genders, sexual orientations, races, ethnicities, religions, social classes, and geographical origins, we can become sufficiently objective to increase the common good and social justice—ideals in our new cultures and new futures.

Social Realities of Societies

Social realities of societies both limit and liberate us. We are born into societies, and this remains one of our most fundamental sources of our personal and social identities. Even though we may identify with particular regions within our current societies—or have traveled so much that that the geographical accidents of our births are no longer significant— the societies in which we were raised often remain more familiar to us than the new countries we adopt as adults.

Having been influenced most by the major characteristics of those societies where we were raised to be adults, we need to reflect and come to terms with the extent to which these experiences direct our actions today. How do cultural values that we absorbed from our original societies influence our perspectives on ourselves, others, our communities, our societies, and globalization?

After acknowledging the social realities that we are members of particular societies, we need to assess their impacts on our cultural preferences. Although we cannot change the facts of our places of birth, we can change the extent to which our local cultures influence our experiences. We can choose to become more educated, for example, which allows us to understand diverse cultures and societies, and enriches our value choices.

In considering the cultural impacts of our past and present societies, we acknowledge the historical influences of our societies on our cultural choices. Living in particular societies means that we adapt to the political and economic conditions of these societies, as well as to their political and economic cultures. When societies are at war, for example, or in economic depressions, our daily experiences and cultural choices are more restricted than during times of peace and prosperity. These are social and cultural consequences of social realities in our societies.

The ranges of variability in societies' circumstances and experiences make the historical accidents of our births dramatically different. In spite of globalization, our lives contrast with each other depending on the countries where we were born or raised. However, these social realities are modified more today than in previous historic times, because increased international communications and travel make migrations more possible for more people. Nevertheless, our relatively recent global social realities do not neutralize the social realities of particular societies, but rather make more individual and social choices possible. For example, when we use social intelligence to understand social facts in our societies more fully, our enlightened value choices help us to improve cultural and social conditions.

Currents of migration are critical aspects of present day globalization. We are more aware that market forces in the global economy are social realities of our international community, and that globalization is accompanied by increases in both legal and illegal international migrations. These complex social realities of globalization move on many fronts, so that the impacts of globalization are experienced in both traditional and modern societies. Consequently, we cannot responsibly deny these historical and global social realities if we are to adapt successfully to our cultures and societies.

Social intelligence suggests that we are strongest when we maintain broad social perspectives and objectivity while adapting to globalization in our societies and cultures. These strategies are viable, because they allow us to be both flexible and versatile in accepting changes in globalization and new value choices. When we choose to stay informed about societal and global social realities, we increase our social intelligence and assume more thoughtful responsibilities as historical actors. For example, if we read serious newspapers and pay attention to fact-based media reports, we keep in touch with our cultures as well as our societies amidst the complex globalization that transforms our worlds.

Although we are increasingly subjected to the strong impacts of globalization, our societies remain as home bases. Social intelligence makes us more aware of how we are related to our societies, or how we can build new societal connections through our value choices and interactions. Social intelligence also shows us that we can choose to be different from our societies, or we can integrate ourselves in our changing societies.

Conforming to our cultures and societies may not always be our wisest choice, even though we need to be recognized as good citizens to achieve self respect and some degree of social honor. Rather, social intelligence encourages us to balance our lives, so that we understand both local and global dynamics in history, and assume responsibilities for bringing about cultural and social changes to solve some of the world's most damaging social problems.

Social Realities and Social Justice

In addition to being found in the five major social influences of families, beliefs, social classes, cultures, and societies, social realities and cultures exist in social justice. Social justice is an important goal of social intelligence, rather than part of the families, beliefs, social classes, cultures, and societies knowledge base of social intelligence. Social justice is also a cultural ideal we work toward when we are socially intelligent, which makes it a critical part of our complex and powerful cultures. Like cultures, social justice has strong connections with social realities.

Because social justice coordinates socially intelligent actions as collective strategies to achieve constructive goals of cultural and social change, social justice motivates us to accomplish goals that are yet unrealized. However, social justice is strongly influenced by social realities, in that it does not hold out false hopes of unattainable goals, but rather directs us toward much needed goals to correct existing social imbalances. In order to accomplish constructive cultural and social goals, social justice must be informed by social intelligence and social realities, which inspire pragmatic strategies to accomplish significant cultural and social changes.

In these respects, social justice is a practical goal for accomplishing somewhat idealistic changes in families, communities, societies, and globalization. For example, social justice inspires effective pragmatic individual and collective strategies. Socially intelligent directions in cultural and social changes are expressed as social justice, which necessarily includes issues about the complex and powerful influences of families, beliefs, social classes, cultures, and societies.

However, social justice is a moral ideal because it is independent from the knowledge base of social intelligence. Although social justice is directly related to problematic social conditions in the influential social spheres of families, beliefs, social classes, cultures, and societies, social justice is not determined by these five major social influences or their social realities.

Social justice reflects possibilities for constructive social realities that express the balance and inclusiveness of this cultural ideal and value choice. Social justice is also a cluster of ideals and values that have distinctive religious and secular traditions. This vast reservoir of cultural ideas and knowledge inspires our individual and collective actions on a daily basis.

The strong moral content of social justice attracts the hearts, minds, and actions of people who want to bring better futures into being. Although these individuals and groups may or may not be aware of their social intelligence, when they learn how to deliberately use socially intelligent principles, the ideals of social justice are more likely to be realized.

Much of the power of the cultural ideals of social justice is directly connected to the social facts of our circumstances.

XI. Social Realities and Cultures

Social justice distinguishes between social conditions that are livable, and those that are unacceptable because they do not allow individuals and groups to survive or thrive. The moral ideal of social justice also focuses on social conditions such as freedom, which is necessary for creating better futures. At the same time, social justice points out social failures and flaws that make us more aware of the power and complexity of the social influences and social realities of families, beliefs, social classes, cultures, and societies.

Because social justice is a cultural and moral ideal, its values cannot be definitively realized through history. Social justice for ever remains unattained, given the nature of human nature, as well as the cultural and social conditions we create as we struggle to survive and be fulfilled. However, social justice is particularly valuable for individuals and groups who are socially intelligent, because this moral ideal sustains their historic efforts—from generation to generation—to achieve more humane and more inspired cultural and social conditions through the common good.

Social justice is rooted in some significant social realities, such as what populations think our improved futures could be. Unlike religious cultural ideals, social justice is not focused on life after death, moral sanctions, or ultimate spiritual fulfillment. Rather, social justice focuses on the social and cultural conditions of our lives in the present and future. Social justice also helps us to organize our efforts to bring improved social conditions into being, because it relates to cultural and social realities of the past, present, and future as well as to moral ideals.

XII. Choosing Cultures

When we are socially intelligent, we realize that we choose our cultures. Even though we are not able to control how new cultural values and ideals enter into our existing cultures, we can control cultures' influences on us to some extent by choosing which cultural values and beliefs we entertain, nurture, and express in our everyday activities.

In some ways cultures also choose us, in that we are identified as being particular individuals depending on the cultural cues that we and others use. For example, our genders, sexual orientations, races, ethnicities, social classes, education, and health or ablebodiedness influence how others see us amidst the cultural maelstroms of our societies and globalization. However, when we persist in making our own choices of cultures, we may neutralize or negate how others see us in our shared cultures.

Becoming more socially intelligent often makes us interested in solving problems related to our situations, or in surviving the push and pull of family responsibilities more comfortably. Sooner or later, however, the broad perspectives of social intelligence shed light on other aspects of our lives, and we may be motivated to make broad changes. One of the ways to accomplish effective changes, through applying the principles of social intelligence, is to choose our cultures. Choosing our cultures is essentially a first step in opening up deeper aspects of our understanding and actions in our everyday lives.

We choose cultures in varied ways. First we realize not only the extent of our cultural choices, but also the limits of our cultural choices. Whatever we choose to emphasize as our most significant values takes on a life of its own. Consequently, our most significant value choices become vehicles of cultural and social changes in their own right. For these reasons we keep our fingers on the pulses of our cultures, so that we make as many deliberate value choices as possible.

Social intelligence helps us to recognize both the significance and the limitations of our cultural and value choices. When we use the broad perspectives of social intelligence—families, beliefs, social classes, cultures, and societies—to understand which cultures and societies we choose, we develop cultural and social strategies which embody constructive cultural and value choices. Because our cultures are ever growing masses of ideals, ideas, knowledge, and beliefs, we must at the same time realize that our cultures are limited by the content of their ideals, ideas, knowledge, and beliefs. Although cultures necessarily remain open to new cultural values, no matter how much societies may try to bar new values politically, societies are inevitably limited by their own dominant ongoing values.

It is difficult to clarify our visions for the future, but our cultures provide wide ranges of symbols for meaningful communications. For example, we create better futures from the present through communications about future cultures based on our past and present cultures. Social intelligence guides us to critically assess our past and present cultures, so that we move into future cultures with social facts that ground our past and present cultural or social realities. Furthermore, when we add precision to our visions of future cultures, and apply the principles of social intelligence to our carefully defined starting points and goals, we are more likely to accomplish our objectives, because we are more effective in implementing strategies that move us in constructive directions.

Ideally we follow the social intelligence principle of working with others to achieve cultural and social changes. Sometimes we find already organized social movements to support our individual efforts to bring about cultural changes. For example, social movements organize around cultural concerns like achieving civil rights or preserving the environment. However, sometimes we must deliberately seek out like-minded others who are committed to changing similar aspects of our cultures and societies. For instance, we may choose to associate with those who cooperate meaningfully with us in designing and implementing socially intelligent strategies to increase the quality of education for members of lower social classes.

Although it is easy to be overwhelmed by the power and complexities of our cultures, especially by enduring traditions, we gradually realize that our lives are inevitably rooted in our cultures. For example, we are human because we are cultural beings. We deal effectively with the seeming eternity of our cultures, when we deliberately use past cultures to understand present cultures. Furthermore, we see options for creating better cultures in the future when we are fully aware of present cultures as well as future possibilities.

Cultures Beget Cultures

Our cultures predictably spawn new cultures, or incorporate selected aspects of outsiders' cultures. Although our cultures have some coherence and internal integrity, they incorporate new symbols, meanings, and ideas into their original cultures, or migrate from one culture to another. Because it is difficult to make laws that create new cultures in democratic societies, we usually decide to nurture the growth of new cultures in less direct ways. For example, we choose to create new cultures, rather than allow ourselves to be coerced to accept new cultures in extraordinary circumstances such as economic depressions or war.

New cultures develop from accumulated value choices. Even though we may try to change some cultural behavior through implementing new laws, it usually takes a long time for new cultures to be accepted or thrive from value choices initiated by legislative changes. Moreover, throughout societies' ongoing cultural and social processes, which both accept and resist cultural changes, external cultures continue to influence our cultures, as well as impact populations' ways of life through individual or family lifestyles.

These social facts about the complexities of changing cultures do not mean that cultures cannot be manipulated. On the contrary, cultures are particularly vulnerable to pressures from commercial interests, or the coercion of those who wield political force. Therefore, social intelligence suggests that as citizens of modern democracies we need to pay attention to our cultures and cultural preferences in order to preserve what is best in our societies and civilizations, so that we create better futures.

Social intelligence shows us that we contribute directly to nurturing healthy, constructive cultures through our value choices. For example, when we support alternative cultural values—such as equality, inclusiveness, diversity, cooperation, and openness—we increase probabilities that we survive and are fulfilled. Furthermore, when we persist in nurturing democratic value choices and social conditions, nations are stronger in their own right.

If cultures are exploited by economic or political special interests, their populations inevitably lose their hold on democratic cultural ideals. Unfortunately, when populations decrease their capacities to make value choices that enhance democratic strengths in their cultures, it is difficult to maintain or rebuild truly democratic communities and societies. Consequently, if we are interested in preserving democratic ideals in our cultures and societies, we need to be engaged in how we make our daily—or hourly—value choices.

Social intelligence helps us to understand the complexities of our cultures, and the impacts that cultures have on significant qualities of our lives. We see that cultures are major social influences in societies, for example, as well as viable ways to bring about constructive cultural and social changes. We also understand that we improve our lives directly through increasing the common good and social justice. We learn—from social intelligence—that we can change our cultures, and that we have responsibilities to change our cultures, in order to sustain life-enhancing impacts on our future societies, civilizations, and globalization.

XII. Choosing Cultures

When we are sufficiently socially intelligent to conduct our lives as responsible historical actors, we recognize the social facts and social realities of our cultures, and change cultures by choosing new cultural values. For example, we choose new cultures at the same time that we shift emphases in our value choices, so that we decide—and make commitments—to embrace alternative values to the current status quo values of our cultures. Examples of these alternative value choices are equality, inclusiveness, diversity, cooperation, and openness. Furthermore, in order to continue to increase our social intelligence, we make alternative cultural and value choices in our everyday behavior.

Social intelligence suggests that an optimal outcome is to have sufficient numbers of people in our societies who care about the power and complexities of our cultures, so that they assume responsibilities for cultural influences by changing their daily value choices. Social intelligence also points out that although we start this process by paying attention to major social and cultural influences, successful outcomes ultimately depend on taking collective constructive actions. For example, we work collectively to formulate new educational policies that express alternative value choices such as equality, inclusiveness, diversity, cooperation, and openness.

Whatever the current cultural preferences of most people are in a given society, we gain much from encouraging cultural and social awareness, and from making more deliberate decisions, commitments, and actions in relation to our cultures. Even when we know that we will not live to see how our cultures and societies change through our new value choices, we are assured that we move societies in life-enhancing directions when we increase social intelligence, the common good, and social justice through our daily actions.

Value Choices as Catalysts

When we view cultural processes from the broad vantage points of social intelligence—families, beliefs, social classes, cultures, and societies—we see that all aspects of the dynamic omnipresence of our complex and powerful cultures are significant. Furthermore, they impact how our societies are as well as how we are. However, we may also ask, through the lens of social intelligence, whether any particular parts of these cultural processes are more significant than the rest. For example, what is most effective—in cultural change processes—in influencing the directions of our cultural and social changes?

Social intelligence recommends that we understand what cultures are, and how cultures have influenced our lives, before we explore specific cultural or social change issues. Social intelligence shows us that we begin to appreciate the power and complexities of cultural and social changes by examining those cultural influences that impact our lives the most. For example, we need to recognize the extent to which our families' cultures, and other cultures, influence how we act, and our ideas about what we would like to change if we could.

It is at this point of examining the impacts of cultures on our everyday lives that we begin to consider the differences that our value choices make. For example, we see that we sometimes set cultural chain reactions in motion by our value choices. Our value choices lead us to select—or not select—particular goals and means to express our chosen values.

Social intelligence helps us to make these powerful but frequently invisible cultural influences more apparent. We begin to assess to what extent we are making our most creative or most productive value choices, for example. We also address which value choices influence how we conduct ourselves most, or how we define our expectations for ourselves, others, and the future.

All in all, our value choices move us in directions that we may or may not prefer. When we choose different values, we go in different directions, as well as use correspondingly different means to achieve our new goals. Consequently, we need to assess to what extent we are accomplishing what we set out to do.

Social intelligence suggests that it is important to understand the crucial nature of our value choices. What we choose as our values makes qualitative differences to us, our families, our communities, our societies, and globalization. For example, we gain power and some social honor through value choices which increase our abilities to select particular goals, and accomplish them individually or collectively.

Social intelligence shows us that we may choose a single cultural value or clusters of values to orient our lives. For example, we may choose to pursue the single value of truth for a lifetime, perhaps by focusing on a scientific truth about a particular environmental or medical problem. This goal leads us to educational programs, career paths, research objectives, specialized professional associations, meaningful family relationships, and the ultimate satisfaction that we discovered or used a new scientific truth to benefit our communities and societies. Thus, social intelligence shows us that making the basic value choice of pursuing scientific truth can transform our lives, and move us toward discovering and revealing scientific truth so that all benefit.

When we choose to focus on a cluster of values, rather than a single value, we have similar outcomes. For example, we may practice one religion for a lifetime, focusing on how the cluster of values in a particular religion inspires individuals and groups to behave responsibly, or participate directly in cultural and social changes. When we do not seek a tangible result from our religious observances and explorations, we frequently gain satisfaction from focusing on trying to understand this religion as much as possible throughout our lives. Also, we may improve our quality of life, as well as the satisfaction and well-being of others, because we choose to live according to this specific cluster of religious values.

Social intelligence pays attention to how we are linked directly to our cultures through our individual and collective value choices. Although we may not have opportunities to formulate cultural and social policies in our societies, we make innumerable value choices each day. We increase our awareness of cultural contacts, meanings, and fulfillment by scrutinizing how we choose our values on a daily basis, and we are more effective—as agents of change—when we choose values that mean the most to us.

We increase our social intelligence by formulating goals that reflect our most cherished values. We also increase the common good and social justice when we are responsible historical actors who make strategic value choices. We know that value choices are significant from the points of view of individual lives and civilizations, and we increase our fulfillment by standing for values that enhance life in current and future civilizations.

Measuring Better Worlds

Even though it is impossible to assess precisely what we want—or think we need—in our future societies and civilizations, we learn from our past cultural experiences that we can design more viable cultural foundations for future societies. However, these new foundations are often little more than well-intentioned directions that reflect our preferred value choices for achieving better worlds tomorrow as well as today.

Social intelligence teaches us that the more precise we are in our visions of improved social conditions, the more likely it is that our plans will come to fruition. We cannot afford to be wishy-washy about what we want to accomplish, for example, if we are to succeed in achieving our goals. When we act on this socially intelligent principle, we move forward decisively because we get to know some important facts about the social situations we want to change.

Examining our cultures closely, as well as distinguishing between traditional and modern cultural values, increases our clarity about future trends and possibilities. For example, we distinguish between cultural values that are constructive or destructive, cultural values that focus on self or collectivities, and cultural values that enhance life rather than lead to death or destruction.

Just as we develop a sense of history by becoming socially intelligent historical actors, we develop a basic knowledge of factual trends and social patterns in order to be more objective in measuring and assessing our current situations and future possibilities. We cannot ignore or deny current facts that define the harshest injustices of social classes, for example. Nor can we allow materialistic values to suffocate our objectivity and moral sensibilities when we have such important matters to decide as which worlds we create for the future.

Cultural values are too important for us not to use them to assess our current situations and future possibilities. We build our worlds of tomorrow through measuring and distinguishing aspects of our social arrangements that have proved beneficial or harmful to our populations. Even when pressures to take responsibility for the next generations of our societies are onerous, it is better to face them and deal with them, than to add to current cultural trends in self-destruction, self-annihilation, or violence. Social intelligence helps us to understand more humane aspects of wars, for example. Furthermore, when we assess the human costs of wars, social intelligence gives us real hope that things can be different.

We learn how to be aware social beings by unlearning unnecessarily destructive aspects of our cultures. We also use social intelligence to design more effective ways to honor constructive cultural value choices, such as cooperation and openness. Placing cooperation and openness at the center of our everyday activities makes it possible to move in more hopeful realistic directions in the present for the future.

Thus social intelligence guides us to make measured assessments of the present and future by emphasizing the importance of objectivity and social facts. Even though our cultures are largely composed of ideas, ideals, and beliefs—that many consider too subjective to understand rationally—we cannot dismiss these vital emotional characteristics as being too difficult to understand objectively, to control, or to direct toward life-enhancing purposes.

Social intelligence helps us to understand the importance of emotions in our families, for example, as well as to appreciate the power and complexity of emotions throughout our cultures and evolution. Consequently, we distinguish patterns in our emotional exchanges and actions, which facilitate making particular value choices.

When we use social intelligence to deal with our ambivalence or extremes in our emotions, we achieve useful results. For example, we measure better future worlds more effectively when we recognize the implications of our current value choices, as well as know which worlds we want to create. Social intelligence deepens our understanding of cultures, so that we identify social facts in both destructive and constructive aspects of our cultures. Furthermore, the precision that flows from these social facts enables us to make decisions and commitments to pursue goals that honor our most constructive values, so that we create better futures.

This simplification of the steps involved in measuring better worlds does not do justice to the ambiguities and frustrations we necessarily encounter in dealing directly with our emotional reactions to others. However, social intelligence shows us that when we stay sufficiently focused on our visions of the future, we can achieve our goals through the assistance of those who share our visions.

Ultimately our visions of the future, however measured, are merely rough blueprints of future possibilities. Above all we cannot afford to lose sight of the major social influences that continue to impact our lives in the present—families, beliefs, social classes, cultures, and societies—as we move toward the future. Furthermore, we must persist in meeting current emotional and cultural needs at the same time that we commit ourselves to move toward better futures.

Choice and Social Movements

Social intelligence teaches us that, in addition to making value choices, we need to work collectively to accomplish our goals as effectively as possible, especially when we are responsible historical actors. For example, when we work with others we address the broader pictures of our lives more adequately, and are more likely to tap into historical and cultural currents of the present. Consequently, our plans for the future are realistic because they are founded on social facts.

In seeking likeminded others to pursue our visions of the future, we frequently start by approaching people we know, such as relatives, friends, acquaintances, colleagues, or friends of friends. We may also contact organizations whose members are committed to social causes which reflect our own values and interests. If we want to work with others in more formal ways, we can join special interest groups, rather than build our own networks, so that our goals merge with the goals of established organizations.

Another viable option, to increase the social impacts of our socially intelligent individual efforts to bring about changes for the future, is to participate in contemporary social movements that head in the same directions. When we are aware or our cultural value choices, we not only identify organizations that have similar goals, but we find groups which are loosely organized around particular value change issues. For example, Internet resources help us to consolidate background information about social movements in modern industrial societies, so that we become better informed about our options.

Social intelligence heightens our awareness about the dangers of sabotaging our intentions to bring about constructive cultural and social changes by working with people who divert our attention away from our goals. We need to stay independent and stalwart in our goal-directed endeavors, sometimes by reminding ourselves about the power of family dependency issues. For example, our social intelligence is based on how we gain independence in our intense family emotional systems. Furthermore, only when we know how to relate to family members with autonomy, can we transfer these skills to varied social settings.

Because social movements are often organized around strengthening particular cultural values, they tend to address alternative cultural values such as equality, inclusiveness, diversity, cooperation, or openness. When social movements take stands which challenge established cultural values like competition, for example, they try to establish social relations that express cooperation. Participants in social movements work cooperatively with each other, rather than in traditional or conventional competitive styles. This helps their messages about the value choice of cooperation to be heard, because we are more likely to bring about changes in our value choices when we express these new values in everyday situations.

Our cultures inspire the wide varieties of symbolic communications that social movements make with general publics. Dance and music may accompany political protests or demonstrations, for example, which add playfulness to serious cultural communications about the benefits of specific cultural and social changes. Thus when we aim to bring inclusiveness and diversity into societies' mainstreams, we may use specific symbols to accomplish this cultural goal.

Religions have some of the same characteristics as social movements, even though they usually use rituals and constantly need to recruit new members. Religions are more specific about their membership requirements than social movements, often insisting that clusters of religious values are accepted rather than secular goals. Nevertheless, social intelligence can guide us to work effectively with either social movements or religious groups in order to meet our shared goals to promote specific community or national changes.

All in all, social intelligence requires us to work with others if we are to be effective in reaching our goals of changing cultures. Social intelligence gives us appropriate tools to achieve emotional maturity, so that making collective efforts is not problematic for us or our cultural causes. For example, when we maintain objectivity—through applying the broad perspectives of families, beliefs, social classes, cultures, and societies in our actions—we can withstand the diversions that participating in social movements sometimes bring. When we aim to increase our social intelligence and strive to be effective and responsible historical actors, we are anchored in social facts and social realities that clarify our visions of present and future possibilities.

Eternal Cultures

Cultures include all our historical records of human accomplishments, as well as all forms of wisdom, literature, arts, music, dance, rhetoric, manifestos, sciences, knowledge, languages, and dreams. We are swamped by cultures, and yet our cultural choices are necessarily limited—by our lifetimes and our capacities to absorb others' cultures as well as those into which we were born.

Our cultures refresh us, and enable us to communicate with some people at considerable depths of meaning. In addition to the refinements and specializations that we learn in modern industrial societies, our cultures allow us to develop senses of universality. For example, we realize that we share basic human experiences, as members of families and communities, with those who are very unlike ourselves. Also, even though we may belong to particular religions, which seem very different from each other, religions give us meanings and symbols that may become integral parts of our universal individual and social identities.

We are born into cultures and die in cultures. Furthermore, all our everyday experiences—and those of our ancestors—are influenced by the power and complexities of our cultures. Although we may choose to have nothing to do with our cultures, even the most reclusive individuals dress, eat, and dream in cultural styles. Thus we both inhale and exhale our cultures whether we realize it or not, and whether we want to or not.

Given the omnipresent power and complexities of our cultures, our adaptations as human beings are largely cultural. For example, we learn languages in order to speak and communicate with others, as well as to express ourselves in our work and leisure activities. We also become aware of how we think through our languages. Furthermore, because we formulate our goals through cultural symbols and meanings, our life satisfaction depends on how we use our cultural resources.

Social intelligence helps us to be objective about the power and complexities of our cultures without diminishing cultural meanings. Rather, social intelligence focuses on the cultural processes we enter into when we interact with others, and when we conduct our everyday business as members of families, communities, and societies. We need cultures in order to be ourselves, and in order to have human relationships. For example, social intelligence guides us to cultivate constructive cultures in our most vital social networks, so that we think and act creatively and effectively.

Even though social intelligence sees cultures as only one of the five major social influences we need to consider in understanding ourselves and our worlds—families, beliefs, social classes, cultures, and societies—cultures are central in bringing about individual and social changes. We increase our objectivity by immersing ourselves in different aspects of our cultures, with the result that we can then design alternative ways of being and doing more effectively.

Social intelligence considers our cultures to be our most significant sources of individual and social innovations. Although we may be compelled to adapt to force, coercion, power, exploitation, or oppression in our particular situations, when we have sufficient freedom and autonomy cultural changes are often our most effective ways to initiate new value choices. For example, cultural changes reorganize or redesign our priorities, so that the foundations and fabrics of our societies are gradually rebuilt.

Social intelligence helps us to appreciate that in many respects our cultures are eternal. Cultures were already present at the dawn of civilizations, because customs and traditions supported our earliest families, tribes, and communities. Even though the values of many of these groups may be considered barbaric, their cultures continued to grow and diversify through time to the present. Furthermore, when we deliberately plan our futures now, we resort to cultural ways of doing things. Therefore, our cultures are frequently our most significant starting points for designing new modes of operating in both local and global social contexts.

The depth and breadth of cultural influences are overwhelming, and cannot be grasped easily. However, the social fact that cultures reflect longstanding values—as well as more recent values—reassures us that we can design cultural changes in thoughtful and knowledgeable ways. We do what we can to survive and be fulfilled through our richest cultural means, because cultural resources have supported and inspired societies throughout history.

The particular ways in which we make cultural changes depend on our social intelligence. For example, we may take things for granted and passively go with the flow of others' cultural changes, or we may take charge of our own cultural destinies by actively selecting cultural values. When we increase our social intelligence, we understand more clearly how we can participate most usefully in these processes. Moreover, we are full participants in cultural processes when we are responsible historical actors who increase the common good and social justice.

From Present to Future

Social intelligence helps us to take safer, more enlightened journeys from the present to the future. Because social intelligence fortifies us with broad cultural perspectives and strategies, we can more securely initiate better futures based on the constructive value choices of equality, inclusiveness, diversity, cooperation, and openness. In addition, we stay hopeful in our efforts to achieve these goals and value choices, because social intelligence shows us how to go forward without becoming pawns in others' exploitation or oppression.

When we travel between the present and the future, we stay informed about our pasts. We are more effective as free and independent travelers on these journeys to the future when we become responsible historical actors. This helps us to balance our knowledge about the past, present, and future in our actions, and in leading others. However, because the past is always with us as strong ongoing cultural influences that we sometimes take for granted, we often feel more influenced by cultural and social facts in the present when we make decisions and commitments about the future.

The power and complexities of our cultures are means to create the future, as well as sources to inspire innovations. We relate to different time dimensions through our cultures, for example, and stay motivated in our purposes to bring about constructive cultural changes for the future, because we build on some of our most significant cultural roots of the past. We embrace both local and global realities through our cultures, in order to maintain depth and breadth in our perspectives during our journeys from the present to the future.

Although some past traditions and long-standing value choices are inevitably perpetuated in the future, we stay focused on alternative value choices in order to bring them into our families, beliefs, social classes, cultures, and societies. For example, we need to know in advance how to be equal and inclusive in our being and doing, as well as how to embrace cultural and social diversity. We also need to make sure that our exchanges with others are cooperative and open rather than competitive and restrictive.

These new cultural emphases are models of how we can live fully in socially intelligent ways. For example, we raise our children and teach members of younger generations to respect the power and complexities of cultural and social processes. We also show through our actions that making decisions and commitments to bring about constructive cultural and social changes is a satisfying goal, which needs to be reinforced by the decisions and commitments of others who pursue goals for the future as well as the present. Thus, passing on socially intelligent knowledge and know-how is a significant aspect of accomplishing meaningful cultural and social changes.

XII. Choosing Cultures

Choosing our cultures is an important part of changing our cultures, and changing our cultures is a significant way to change societies. We are who we are because of the cultural resources available to us, and we move from the present to better futures when we make more deliberate and more enlightened value choices. These existential conditions influence the qualities of our survival and fulfillment. Ultimately, our decisions and commitments about our value choices enable us to move successfully from the present to better futures.

In a rapidly changing world with increasing globalization, we must strategize as carefully as possible about our options for creating better futures from the present. Social intelligence is a tool that helps us in this endeavor, as well as a means that strengthens our contributions to the common good and social justice. However, we cannot achieve what needs to be done as individuals in pursuit of individual goals. We are more effective when we work cooperatively with others, and finding our collective voice is one of our most significant tasks in journeying from the present to better futures.

We need to know not only the changes we want in the future and how to make them, but also with whom we should work to achieve our goals. For example, mass education makes it possible to communicate meaningfully with large groups of people, so that the Internet facilitates both national and international communications. Although working with others brings its own challenges and difficulties, social intelligence reminds us that we are compelled to create ways to cooperate effectively. We cannot work alone to create improved futures, because we must depend on others to meet these goals.

Therefore, we necessarily pioneer cooperative, collective work styles as well as innovative cultural value choices. For example, we forge our ways from the present to the future with relationships and communications that are sufficiently strong to deal with everyday stresses. Social intelligence also teaches us how to deal with the resistance of those who do not choose to make creating better futures a priority.

Cultures and Social Intelligence

We use social intelligence to give us reliable knowledge about how to achieve freedom as we work together, so that we do not stifle others with our demands. Consequently, social intelligence principles guide us to work side by side as free independent individuals, who are headed in the same or similar directions.

Social intelligence continues to guide us in our journeys from the present to the future. For example, social intelligence enlightens our assessments of our starting points, especially with regard to particular situations in our families, beliefs, social classes, cultures, and societies. This allows us to gradually embrace equality, inclusiveness, diversity, cooperation, and openness as alternative cultural choices. Lastly, social intelligence encourages us to use our cultures in these worthwhile endeavors, so that cultural meanings, processes, and ideals become inspirations, supports, and reinforcements for improved futures.

Suggested Reading

Amato, Paul R., Alan Booth, David R. Johnson, and Stacy J. Rogers. 2007. *Alone Together: How Marriage in America is Changing.* Cambridge, MA: Harvard University Press.

Benedict, Ruth. 1934. *Patterns of Culture.* Boston, MA: Houghton Mifflin.

Berger, Peter L. 1963. *Invitation to Sociology.* New York, NY: Doubleday.

Berger, Peter L., and Thomas Luckmann. 1966. *The Social Construction of Reality.* New York, NY: Doubleday.

Bernard, Jessie. 1987. *The Female World from a Global Perspective.* Bloomington, IN: Indiana University Press.

Bowen, Murray. 1978. *Family Therapy in Clinical Practice.* New York: Jason Aronson.

Du Bois, W. E. B. 1994/1903. *The Souls of Black Folk.* New York, NY: Dover Publications.

Epstein, Cynthia Fuchs. 1988. *Deceptive Distinctions: Sex, Gender, and the Social Order.* New Haven, CT: Yale University Press.

Gans, Herbert J. 1999. *Popular Culture and High Culture: An Analysis and Evaluation of Taste.* New York, NY: Basic Books.

Gardner, Howard. 1983. *Multiple Intelligences.* New York, NY: Basic Books.

Giddens, Anthony. 1999. *Runaway World: How Globalization is Shaping our Lives.* London: Profile Books.

Gitlin, Todd. 2002. *Media Unlimited: How the Torrent of Images and Sounds Overwhelms Our Lives.* New York, NY: Metropolitan Books.

Goffman, Erving. 1959. *The Presentation of Self in Everyday Life.* Garden City, NY: Doubleday.

Kerr, Michael E., and Murray Bowen. 1988. *Family Evaluation.* New York: W. W. Norton.

Lorber, Judith. 1993. *Paradoxes of Gender.* New Haven, CT: Yale University Press.

Manders, Dean Wolfe. 2006. *The Hegemony of Common Sense: Wisdom and Mystification in Everyday Life.* New York, NY: Peter Lang.

Mills, C. Wright. 1959. *The Sociological Imagination.* New York, NY: Oxford University Press.

Morgan, Kimberly J. 2006. *Working Mothers and the Welfare State: Religion and the Politics of Work-Family Policies in Western Europe and the United States.* Palo Alto, CA: Stanford University Press.

Prather, Jane Emery. 2006. *Brave New Stepfamilies: Diverse Paths Toward Stepfamily Living.* Thousand Oaks, CA: Sage Publications.

Reisman, David. 1961. *The Lonely Crowd: A Study of the Changing American Character.* New Haven, CT: Yale University Press.

Shupe, Anson. 2007. *Spoils of the Kingdom: Clergy Misconduct and Religious Community.* Champagne, IL: University of Illinois Press.

Wilson, William J. 1987. *The Truly Disadvantaged: The Inner City, the Underclass, and Public Policy.* Chicago, IL: University of Chicago Press.

Wuthnow, Robert. 1998. *After Heaven: Spirituality in America Since the 1950s.* Berkeley, CA: University of California Press.

With many thanks to my colleagues at Georgetown University Sociology Department, the Bowen Center for the Study of the Family, Association for Applied and Clinical Sociology, and the Commission on Applied and Clinical Sociology. I am also indebted to my clients and students, who have taught me so much, and of course to my wonderful American and English families, who continue to put up with me on a daily basis.